\WILL YOU PICK UP YOUR CROSS AND FOLLOW JESUS?/

James J. Holden
Founder/Mantour Ministries

Ride or Die: Will You Pick Up Your Cross And Follow Jesus?
Copyright © 2021 Mantour Ministries

Published by 4One Ministries, Inc. Visit www.mantourministries.com for more information on bulk discounts and special promotions, or e-mail your questions to info@4oneministries.org.

Design: James J. Holden

Subject Headings:
1. Christian life 2. Men's Ministry 3. Spiritual Growth

ISBN 978-1-7378821-0-7
ISBN 978-1-7378821-1-4 (ebook)
Printed in the United States of America

DEDICATION

This book is dedicated to a group of men that I highly respect and look to for inspiration. These pastors in their sixties and early seventies model daily what it means to ride or die. While many men of this age (and even younger) are waiting for the time they can retire to a life of luxury, these men still ride and die with complete abandon.

- One retired from his pastorate and now drives a school bus every day so he can reach the younger generation. He still does pulpit fill almost every Sunday.

- One retired from his pastorate, but still teaches classes at his church. Shortly after retirement, he began dialysis. But he still ministers, doing counseling sessions over the phone while getting his dialysis treatments.

- One retired from his pastorate, but now started a new ministry traveling around to churches performing dramatic presentations, encouraging people to take tough stands in today's world.

- One is at the age to retire, but, instead of winding down, is planning to expand his church and is constantly looking for ways to grow the church even more while speaking the truth each week.

These four men have a ride or die attitude. Nothing, not even time itself, keeps them from doing what God tells them to do. They are a constant reminder to me that the sacrifices and steps of obedience that God calls me to take are worth it. They inspire me daily to ride or die with God and, like them, hold nothing back. They remind me that retirement is not the finish line; the finish line is eternity. Until then, I choose to follow their lead and ride or die with God, no matter what!

I dedicate this book to Stan Williams, Roland Coon, Walt Smith, and Phil Menditto.

TABLE OF CONTENTS

CHAPTER ONE

RIDE OR DIE? WHAT'S THAT??

I've always been a musical person. My idea of a great day off is sitting in the sun on my back porch listening to music. Our family joke was that I didn't know a car could still run without the radio being on. I love going on car rides, opening the sunroof, and blasting my music as loud as I can. I often joke it's witnessing to blast DCTalk or the Newsboys around town while I run errands.

Music has always spoken to me. I have playlists for everything. I have a bummed playlist for more challenging days. I have a redneck playlist for drives through the country. I have playlists for my two favorite holidays, Christmas and July 4th. A trip to the beach means listening to my beach music playlist. I even have a fried chicken playlist for when I cook my specialty, homemade chicken tenders. Music has always been my go-to means of dealing with a bad day.

Can I be honest with you? 2021 was a pretty rough year for me personally. There were many times this year I played my go-to pick-me-up songs as I dealt with physical, financial, emotional, and spiritual crises.

I remember one particularly tough day. I was supposed to start writing this book, but I really was struggling to get started. Some really tough situations I was facing filled my mind, and I got to the place where I needed to clear my head. I asked Alexa to play something by TobyMac. She chose to play the song *"Ignition."*

I had heard this song a million times before. However, today as I listened, a line from the song JUMPED out the Alexa device and into my ears. If you've never heard the song before, I encourage you to take a listen. The song discusses going through difficult trials and struggles and the need to ignite our spiritual engines and keep going forward. The song encourages you to keep going through your difficulties. In the song, he encourages the listener to persevere and ride or die.

This song expressed perfectly where I was at and how I felt. But the last sentiment really stood out to me the most.

Ride or Die

I had heard this phrase before and never given it much thought, but that day it really stood out to me. So I decided to research it a little bit. According to Dictionary.com, a ride or die is *"a colloquial expression of extreme loyalty to someone or something."*[1] The Urban Dictionary defines *"ride or die"* as *"when you are willing to do anything for someone you love or someone you really appreciate in your life. You ride or die for the person who stood by you in any problem and vice versa."*[2]

So basically, to *"ride or die"* means you will do anything for the person you love. There is nothing they could ask of you that you would not be willing to do. It means you will go to the ends of the earth for them, take risks for them, you will stand by them no matter the cost. You will ride with them even if it ends up killing you. It's a statement of extreme loyalty and devotion to someone else.

As I read this, something inside of me broke. I instantly remembered a passage of Scripture from Matthew 16:24-26:

> *Then Jesus said to his disciples, "Whoever wants to be my disciple must deny themselves and take up their cross and follow me. For whoever wants to save their life will lose it, but whoever loses their life for me will find it. What good will it be for someone to gain the whole world, yet forfeit their soul? Or what can anyone give in exchange for their soul?" (NIV)*

To spiritually ride or die means we have to pick up our cross for Jesus. Even when it's hard. Even when we don't like what God is choosing to do with our lives. Even when we are facing hard times. Even when the future may not look so bright. As God's sons, we need to be saying to Him in the dark, difficult times, *"I'm still committed to You. I will follow You through the good times and even the bad. I will ride or die with You!"*

As God's sons, we need to be saying to Him in the dark, difficult times, "I'm still committed to You. I will follow You through the good times and even the bad. I will ride or die with You!"

Can I be completely open and honest with you? I mean, really, really honest. Not *"make Jamie look good,"* honest?

At this moment, I realized that I was struggling because I was not spiritually and physically strong enough to help anyone. I started to realize that over the past six or seven months, I had become wiped out. I was exhausted. I wasn't burnt out from ministry. I was exhausted from things that had been happening in my own life over the past number of months.

As we ended 2020 and entered 2021, God decided to put a stick of dynamite on my life, and it exploded. We experienced HUGE life changes in health, finances, and actual day-to-day life. God uprooted our lives in ways I never saw coming, I never expected, and, honestly, hated. I wasn't expecting it. I didn't like it, and dealing with all of this while in the heart of our Mantour season left me mentally, emotionally, and spiritually exhausted.

Can I be even more honest? I never experienced the temptation to walk away from my life and ministry as I did at this time in my life. I just couldn't believe what was going on around me. I spent most of my prayer time saying to God, *"What happened? How did we get here? How are You going to fix it?"*

But then Alexa played this song, and things came into focus. After researching the meaning of the term ride or die, I knew what I had to do.

I had to come to the place where I chose to ride or die for God. I had a very honest talk with God where I said, *"I honestly can't see why You are doing what You are doing. I don't like it. I really wish You would do something different. BUT EVEN IF YOU DON'T, I will ride or die with You. I will go through this season You have put us in. I may not know what You are doing and why You are doing it, but I am wholeheartedly committed to You!"*

As soon as I reached this place of surrender, I began to see what God wanted this book to be, and I was able to start writing. I always say I end up living whatever the following year's Mantour theme will be (Adessa wants to do a beach resort theme in 2023!) before we share it with the men, and this year was no exception.

I firmly believe I am not alone. I don't know where you are at right now. I don't know what you're going through. Maybe you are flying high and see smooth skies ahead. Perhaps you are facing some struggles and are persevering through. Maybe you are so deep in the mire that you feel stuck and see no way out. No matter where you are or what you are facing, I believe God has a challenge for you to take in your life. He wants to ask you, *"Will you ride or die with Me?"*

Will you ride or die with Him if He takes your perfect life and turns it upside down?

How about if what He asks you to do goes against the cultural norms? What if He asks you to stand for something the Twitter mob won't like?

What if He asks you to go in a completely different direction in your career or calling?

Will you commit to ride or die if He shakes your comfort zone?

What about if He asks you to take a ginormous leap of faith for Him?

It's easy to say, *"I will ride or die for God"* when everything is going great.   But when the going gets tough, will you get riding?

I don't want you to think choosing to ride or die with God means you are doomed to face hard, difficult times. You can ride or die through the good times as well. The second part of the Urban dictionaries definition of *"Ride or Die"*

says:

"The "ride" doesn't always have to be a negative either. Obviously, if you're this close to someone, you want them to enjoy the "ride" (life and all it has to offer) with them as well."[2]

God wants us to ride with Him in the good and the bad. It is basically a life choice to make that you are committed and loyal to God every day and in every circumstance.

In this book, I want to challenge and encourage you that there really is no better way to live than a life devoted to God. No matter what we are going through, we need to have a ride or die attitude with God. We need to decide that there is nothing God could ask of you that you would not be willing to do. It means you will go to the ends of the earth for Him, take risks for Him, you will stand by Him and for Him no matter the cost. You will ride with Him even if it ends up killing you. By the end of this book, I hope you will do what I described earlier…make a statement of extreme loyalty and devotion to God, no matter what He does, where He leads, or what He asks of you.

Each chapter of this book will focus on the stories of the heroes of the faith who had gone before us, men who choose to ride or die for God in the face of lions, fiery furnaces, religious hypocrites, social pressures, and a host of other circumstances. These men were real guys, just like you or me. They had strengths as well as a whole lot of weaknesses and flaws. Each one of them had to make hard choices to ride or die with God. I hope their stories inspire you to make the choices they made, that no matter what they encountered, what trials they faced, or whatever God required of them, they would ride or die with Him!

As always, each chapter will have group study questions so that you can work through them with a group of men. I STRONGLY encourage you to do this. We have been blown away by the testimonies of how God has worked through these books as men worked through them together in their men's ministry. There is strength in numbers. Work together with other men and choose to ride or die together. The book also includes a workbook so you can go more in-depth personally as well as be a format for discussion in your small group.

Are you ready to go? Let's start our journey together as we learn to ride or die with God!

Group Study Questions:

1. What does the phrase, *"Ride or Die"* mean spiritually?

2. This chapter stated, *"To spiritually ride or die means we have to pick up our cross for Jesus."* What is your reaction to this statement?

3. What is your greatest fear when it comes to picking up your cross and following Jesus?

4. Is this fear rational? Or would it not be as bad as you think?

5. After reading this chapter, what is one thing you will put into practice or one thing you will change in your life?

6. How can we, as a group, help you do this?

CHAPTER TWO

RIDE OR DIE OBEDIENTLY

*Noah was a righteous man, blameless among the people of his time, and
he walked faithfully with God.*

*H*ave you ever been on a cruise? My friends are always telling me,
"Jamie, you need to go on a cruise. You'd love it." My answer is always
the same... *"NO THANKS!"*

Other than the obvious expense of a cruise, there are strong
reasons I wouldn't want to go on a cruise ship. Even before the
Covid-19 pandemic, the news always had stories of people getting
sick on a cruise...yuck. Second, I watched way too many episodes of
Gilligan's Island as a kid and saw what a three-hour tour could turn
into...imagine the results of a bigger ship for a week!

Also, the cabins on *The Love Boat* looked very crowded. I need
my space! Plus, you're miles away from anything on the water. Even

more, ever since 9/11, I have always thought that a cruise ship is a perfect terrorist target to fly a plane into, it's all alone and it would be a while until it was discovered. (Should I worry that I think about good terrorist targets?) Anyway, I'm happy for you if you enjoy a cruise trip. Have a great time, but in my opinion, it isn't for me... you can have them!

Did you know the first cruise ship is mentioned in the Bible? Only this time, instead of a pleasure cruise, it was a life raft for all that God deemed worthy of saving for repopulating the earth, which unfortunately was only eight people and a boat-load of animals. This cruise was a mode of salvation for all mankind, a precursor to Jesus Himself. This boat only came into existence because of the ride or die attitude of one man, Noah. Let's look at what made Noah a man that God would trust with the future of all mankind.

> *The Lord saw how great the wickedness of the human race had become on the earth, and that every inclination of the thoughts of the human heart was only evil all the time. The Lord regretted that he had made human beings on the earth, and his heart was deeply troubled. So the Lord said, "I will wipe from the face of the earth the human race I have created—and with them the animals, the birds and the creatures that move along the ground—for I regret that I have made them." But Noah found favor in the eyes of the Lord. -Genesis 6:5-8, NIV*

Mankind's sinful hearts had taken full root across the earth, and God's holiness couldn't stand the filthy unholiness that took place daily. Judgment was about to fall! However, in His infinite grace, God chose not to annihilate humanity. He saw a small glimmer of light in the middle of the perverse darkness...a man named Noah.

Why did God choose to spare Noah? We read this in the next verses.

Noah was a righteous man, blameless among the people of his time, and he walked faithfully with God. Noah had three sons: Shem, Ham and Japheth. - Genesis 6:9, NIV

The fact that God spared Noah shows He isn't an angry God Who destroys those who displease Him. Instead, it shows He is a loving God Who never wants to destroy people but whose holiness demands judgment for sin. He is so loving that He examined the hearts of all mankind, every person alive. But sadly, the only heart He found that was devoted to Him was Noah.

Even when everyone around him pursued filth and sin, Noah determined to ride or die with God!

When God saw Noah, He didn't see a perfect, sinless man. He saw was a man who strived daily to be as sinless as possible, who obeyed God at all times, and who strived to live for God every minute of every day. Noah made a conscious effort to be different from the evil people around him. He intentionally lived a faithful and obedient life to God. Even when everyone around him pursued filth and sin, Noah determined to ride or die with God!

Now the earth was corrupt in God's sight and was full of violence. God saw how corrupt the earth had become, for all the people on earth had corrupted their ways. So God said to Noah, "I am going to put an end to all people, for the earth is filled with violence because of them. I am surely going to destroy both them and the earth.

So make yourself an ark of cypress wood; make rooms in it and coat it with pitch inside and out. This is how you are to build it: The ark is to be three hundred cubits long, fifty cubits wide and thirty cubits high. Make a roof for it, leaving below the roof an opening one cubit high all around. Put a door in the side of the ark and make lower, middle and upper decks. I am going to bring floodwaters on the earth to destroy all life under the heavens, every creature that has the breath of life in it. Everything on earth will perish.

But I will establish my covenant with you, and you will enter the ark—you and your sons and your wife and your sons' wives with you. You are to bring into the ark two of all living creatures, male and female, to keep them alive with you. Two of every kind of bird, of every kind of animal and of every kind of creature that moves along the ground will come to you to be kept alive. You are to take every kind of food that is to be eaten and store it away as food for you and for them." - Genesis 6:11-21, NIV

God presented Noah with His plan of salvation. He wanted Noah to build an ark to spare the animals and his family from the coming flood from the rain. Now, you have to understand a few things here. First, no one had ever seen a boat before. God told Noah to build a giant ark, a big boat, and I am sure Noah's first answer was, *"Of course God, I'll do whatever You ask, if You want me to build a boat, I'll build You a boat…but just one quick question. What is a boat?"*

Second, you have to know that no one had ever seen rain before. God wanted a boat built to survive the flood-rains that were coming. There was no way Noah could have known what that meant because he had never seen rain before. The earth hadn't experienced rain up until this point; God watered it via a mist. Now He was telling Noah to build a boat which he had never seen because of flooding rain which he had never experienced. How did Noah respond?

Noah did everything just as God commanded him.
- Genesis 6:22, NIV

Even though it made absolutely no sense to Noah, he obeyed God anyway. Why? Because he lived a life of obedience, a life devoted to God, a life that would ride or die with God no matter what. This brings us to our first point.

1. Even when it makes no sense, you still obey.

There is no way in the world that what God asked Noah to do made any sense to him. It DEFINITELY made zero sense to the sinful people all around Noah. These people paid no attention to God. They lived however they pleased and pursued as much sin as possible. Can you imagine the ridicule and persecution Noah received when he started building the ark? I am sure he became known far and wide as *"Crazy Old Noah."*

Think about this. The ark God designed was the length of one and a half football fields. A quick search of the Ark on Wikipedia shows us that the ark was close to the size of the aircraft carrier, the USS Independence. This was a HUGE project being built by basically four guys, Noah and his three boys.

Remember, they didn't have Lowes or Home Depot to buy some cypress wood. They had to cut it down, mill it, and then build it. They didn't have chain saws, drills, or other power tools. They had to build it by hand with hand tools. This project probably took years to complete. That meant for YEARS Noah had to have faith and obedience to stick with the project. For years, he had to keep his sons invested in a project like this. Over many years, he faced the jeers, insults, and persecution of the wicked people all around them. This was not an easy project, it made zero sense, but Noah did it anyway because he strove to live a life of obedience to God.

There will be times in your life where God asks you to do things that make absolutely no sense to you. You see no reason for doing it, and it comes at a tremendous personal cost. At this moment, you have to choose if you will ride or die in obedience or ignore God's will for you.

I remember vividly a time when Adessa and I faced such a situation. In 2019, we both felt separately in our prayer time that God was leading us to take our two-car garage and convert it into office space. At the time, it made zero sense to us why God would want us to do this. Then we got an estimate from a contractor and saw what it would cost, and it REALLY didn't make sense. We didn't have that kind of money! Why would God ask such a thing? But it became clear over time that this is exactly what God wanted. So we obediently walked where God was leading, shaking in fear the entire way...but we still obeyed!

This project cost us every cent we had. Even after very generous donations from churches and individuals for this project (we even had one couple give us a check that they specifically designated to buy a toilet for the room!), it took all of our ministry's funds and all of our personal savings to do this project. We paid a contractor to do the hard stuff like framing, plumbing, and electricity until the money ran out. Then we, along with some friends and a men's ministry team from a local church, finished the work ourselves.

Throughout the entire project, we constantly asked each other, *"Why are we doing this? It makes no sense!"* Each time the answer was the same... *"Because God told us to do it, and our job is to be obedient even if it makes no sense."*

Shortly after the room project was completed and we had our office space, it quickly became apparent why God led us to do this. A few months later, the Covid-19 pandemic rocked the world, and we all were forced to shut down and stay home. There was no way we would have been able to go through this time without the privacy of our office!

Then at the start of 2021, my father, who lives with us, had a medical emergency and was forced to retire. Now he is home all day, bored, and looking for someone to entertain him. We would have never been able to get anything done without the private office God called us to create. It made zero sense at the time, but I am so glad we decided to ride or die in obedience and do what God called us to do.

In your life, there will be times when God asks you to be obedient, and it will make no sense to you at all. The only option you have at this moment is to trust God, roll up your sleeves, and say, *"Even though this makes no sense to me, You know what You are doing, and I will ride or die in obedience to You."*

2. Obedience brings the big job; the big job doesn't bring obedience.

The second thing I want to point out about Noah is this…God didn't ask Noah to obey him and build a boat. God asked Noah to build a boat because he knew Noah lived a life of obedience to Him. Noah's obedience brought him the big job; the big job didn't bring obedience to Noah.

God already knew Noah would do what He asked because He knew Noah had a heart of obedience. He saw Noah's obedience in his past, and He knew Noah could be depended on for even more responsibility. God knew that whatever He asked of Noah, Noah would fist pump Him and say, *"I'm riding or dying with You…no matter what!"* Because of this attitude, Noah was used by God to save the universe from extinction.

You have no idea what your obedience in everyday things could lead to in God's Kingdom. Those small steps of faith in obedience could lead you to life-changing leaps of faith that will change your life as well as those around you for eternity. You must adopt a daily ride or die attitude of obedience so that when God presents the bigger chance for obedience, you won't think twice about riding or dying with him.

God knew that whatever He asked of Noah, Noah would fist pump Him and say, "I'm riding or dying with you...no matter what!"

Sometimes I think we approach God improperly. We enter into prayer and tell God we will do anything if He will just bless us and give us something great or big or set us free of a struggle.

We ask God to use us mightily for His Kingdom, and He says, *"Why don't you start by simply reading the Bible and praying every day?"* We answer, *"I'll do anything for God, but I can't do that."*

We ask God to bless our finances and give us a big promotion at work. God answers, *"How can I promote you and reward you financially when you don't obey Me in your tithes?"* We answer, *"I'd do anything for God, but I can't afford that."*

We want God to make us a big deal in His kingdom, but God says, *"How can I trust you with something big when you won't obey Me in something as small as stop watching ungodly tv shows and movies that promote anti-God ways and principles?"* We say, *"I'd do anything for God, but I can't give up that show."*

Guys, we can't have this attitude when we approach God. We need to do whatever it takes to ride or die in obedience.

- We will do whatever we need to do.

- We will go wherever we need to go.

- We will change whatever we need to change.

- We will confess whatever we need to confess.

We will do whatever is necessary to become everything God called us to be and walk in obedience to Him. Then, like Noah, God will look at you as a man He knows He can trust to take a leap of obedient faith for Him because you have already obeyed Him in the little things.

Noah was such a man, and because of his lifetime of obedience, God used him to save humanity from extinction.

> *The Lord then said to Noah, "Go into the ark, you and your whole family, because I have found you righteous in this generation. Take with you seven pairs of every kind of clean animal, a male and its mate, and one pair of every kind of unclean animal, a male and its mate, and also seven pairs of every kind of bird, male and female, to keep their various kinds alive throughout the earth. Seven days from now I will send rain on the earth for forty days and forty nights, and I will wipe from the face of the earth every living creature I have made."*
>
> *And Noah did all that the Lord commanded him. - Genesis 7:1-5, NIV*

Noah did as the Lord commanded. Why? Because it was how he rolled. He had a life-long ride or die attitude of obedience.

> *On that very day Noah and his sons, Shem, Ham and Japheth, together with his wife and the wives of his three sons, entered the ark... Then the Lord shut him in.*

For forty days the flood kept coming on the earth, and as the waters increased they lifted the ark high above the earth. The waters rose and increased greatly on the earth, and the ark floated on the surface of the water. They rose greatly on the earth, and all the high mountains under the entire heavens were covered... Every living thing that moved on land perished—birds, livestock, wild animals, all the creatures that swarm over the earth, and all mankind. Everything on dry land that had the breath of life in its nostrils died. Every living thing on the face of the earth was wiped out; people and animals and the creatures that move along the ground and the birds were wiped from the earth. Only Noah was left, and those with him in the ark. - Genesis 7:13 and 16-23, NIV

God's judgment fell, and all life was destroyed except Noah and his family. It is sad to see the consequences of a life of sin. But a life of obedience is always rewarded. This brings us to the last point I want to look at in this chapter.

3. You have no idea what your obedience will mean for your children.

God remembered Noah and all the wild animals and the livestock that were with him in the ark, and he sent a wind over the earth, and the waters receded... Then God said to Noah, "Come out of the ark, you and your wife and your sons and their wives. Bring out every kind of living creature that is with you—the birds, the animals, and all the creatures that move along the ground—so they can multiply on the earth and be fruitful and increase in number on it."

So Noah came out, together with his sons and his wife and his sons' wives. All the animals and all the creatures that move along the ground and all the birds—everything that moves on land—came out of the ark, one kind after another. - Genesis 8:1 and 15-19, NIV

Noah, his family, and a boat-load of smelly, hungry, cramped animals spent well over a year in the ark together before the floods receded enough for God to let them leave safely. That's a long time to be on a floating zoo! But God did His part and saved Noah and his family from extinction.

I want to look back at the passage we looked at earlier.

Noah was a righteous man, blameless among the people of his time, and he walked faithfully with God. Noah had three sons: Shem, Ham and Japheth…God saw how corrupt the earth had become, for all the people on earth had corrupted their ways. - Genesis 6:9-10, NIV

Notice it didn't say God saw Noah's three sons as righteous. It just says Noah was righteous. It actually says all the people besides Noah were corrupt. It only stands to reason that since the sons aren't designated as righteous and blameless, they must be included in the *"all the people"* group. But God spared Noah's sons because of their father's righteousness.

Let's finish this passage:

Then Noah built an altar to the Lord and, taking some of all the clean animals and clean birds, he sacrificed burnt offerings on it. The Lord smelled the pleasing aroma and said in his heart: "Never again will I curse the ground because of humans, even though every inclination of the human heart is evil from childhood. And never again will I destroy all living creatures, as I have done. As long as the earth endures, seedtime and harvest, cold and heat, summer and winter, day and night will never cease." - Genesis 8:20-22, NIV

Noah's complete and unabandoned obedience to God caused God to promise never to abandon him and future generations again. He was so impressed by Noah's ride or die attitude that future generations will never experience a world-wide flood again.

Men, you have no idea how your life of riding or dying obediently with God will affect your children. Noah's sons were given another chance at life because their father loved and served God and walked in obedience. They had an opportunity that none of their other friends had, to choose to follow their father's example and live their life for God in obedience.

This should definitely cause us to think about how our obedience can affect future generations. Are you leaving a legacy of ride or die obedience for the next generation to follow? Are you a godly example for them to emulate? I once heard a pastor say, *"One generation's compromise leads to another generation's disobedience."* What a

"One generation's obedience leads to the next generation's victories."

great quote that should cause us to want to live a life of obedience to God. I guess the flip side of this quote would be, *"One generation's obedience leads to the next generation's victories."*

I like that! I want to be a man who inspires the next generation to obey God no matter what He asks and no matter how crazy it may seem. But this only happens when we adopt an attitude of obedience no matter what God asks or where He leads. There is no highway option for a ride or die man of God…the only option is obedience.

Will you choose to become a man who obeys God no matter what?

Will you follow Him even when it makes no sense to you?

Will you obey Him in the small things so He can trust you with bigger things?

Will you be a man of God who leads the next generation with an attitude of obedience?

Will you ride or die obediently for your Savior?

Group Study Questions:

1. Why did God choose Noah to build the ark?

2. Has God ever asked you to do something that, to you, made absolutely no sense? Did you do it? What was the result?

3. This chapter made the point: *"Obedience brings the big job; the big job doesn't bring obedience."* What does this mean to you?

4. Are there any times where you don't respond properly when God asks you to do something? What changes do you need to make?

5. How can your obedience or disobedience affect your children?

6. After reading this chapter, what is one thing you will put into practice or one thing you will change in your life?

7. How can we, as a group, help you do this?

CHAPTER THREE

RIDE OR DIE BY OVERCOMING

..Thomas…said to the rest of the disciples, "Let us also go, that we may die with him".

Last night we had some REALLY bad storms where I live in Pennsylvania. It was so windy, the lightning was magnificent, and the cool breeze from the storm was a welcome relief from the summer heat.

As the storm blew through, it took with it our internet and cable. Thankfully, we didn't lose power, but we had no wifi or tv service. Having had a long day of writing the previous chapter and then recording podcasts the remainder of the day, I was tired and just wanted to flop in front of the tv and unwind.

Thankfully, I had some movies downloaded onto a portable external hard drive. Adessa picked a Hallmark movie (of course), and then I picked an old Adam Sandler movie, *"Bedtime Stories,"* afterward. As I was watching the movie Adessa picked, someone in the movie said, *"I don't trust anyone without a nickname."*[1]

That line struck me funny. However, it really fits into what I am going to write about today. A good nickname is a great thing. *Honest Abe, Richard the Lion Heart, Alexander the Great, Megatron, "The Rock" Duane Johnson, Hammerin' Hank Williams, Iron Mike Tyson*, those are AWESOME nicknames.

A bad nickname isn't such a great thing. Take, for instance, names like *Ivan the Terrible, Louis "Do-Nothing" V King of France, Slick Willy, and the Washington football team…*these names are terrible nicknames!

In this chapter, I want to look at a man who may have landed the worst nickname in history. In my opinion, he didn't deserve the label. He was a man who chose to ride or die with Jesus, and he never wavered on this claim. However, because his personality was cautious and somewhat pessimistic, glass-half-empty kinda guy, he never gets the credit he deserves for being the amazing man he was. He overcame his personality traits and became a true-blue, dyed in the wool follower of Jesus. Let's look at the life of Thomas.

Thomas was one of the twelve men blessed with the greatest internships in history, being one of Jesus' disciples. Not much is known about Thomas' history. The Bible doesn't focus on that part of his life. All we really know is he must have had a twin brother or sister because John 11 says he was also known as *Didymus*, which means *"twin"* in Greek. However, his nickname of *"the twin"* was replaced with the name *"Doubting Thomas"* for all history because of his pessimistic personality, and particularly because he couldn't wrap his grief-stricken, broken-hearted mind around the possibility that Jesus had risen. He hadn't yet seen Jesus alive after the crucifixion, and he wanted to see it for himself. Yes, that was Thomas' natural disposition, but to label him with it forever isn't fair, in my opinion, as we will see in the passage we will examine. Instead, I think he should be called *"Overcoming Thomas"*!

As I said, we don't know much about Thomas' past pre-Jesus. What we do know about Thomas is that when Jesus called him, he answered the call. He followed Jesus daily, riding or dying with Him. He sat daily with Jesus and learned from Him. He probably told stories about *"the one that got away"* while fishing with Jesus. He probably joked around the campfire with Jesus and the other disciples on a regular basis. He got to do what millions throughout history wish they had the chance to do: walk and talk with Jesus.

While we don't know a lot about his past, the passages focused on him show us his personality. He was devoted and loyal to Jesus. He went wherever Jesus went. While many of Jesus' disciples were loud, brash, and sometimes foolish, this is not how the Bible portrays Thomas. The stories of his personality often show him as more pessimistic, less likely to be the boldest and out-front kind of guy. Honestly, you wouldn't expect him to be a ride or die type of man. But he was. His love and devotion for God helped him conquer his natural tendencies and become a true ride or die disciple. How do I know this? Let's look at John chapter 11 together.

> *Now a man named Lazarus was sick. He was from Bethany, the village of Mary and her sister Martha. (This Mary, whose brother Lazarus now lay sick, was the same one who poured perfume on the Lord and wiped his feet with her hair.) So the sisters sent word to Jesus, "Lord, the one you love is sick."*
>
> *When he heard this, Jesus said, "This sickness will not end in death. No, it is for God's glory so that God's Son may be glorified through it." Now Jesus loved Martha and her sister and Lazarus. So when he heard that Lazarus was sick, he*

stayed where he was two more days, and then he said to his
disciples, "Let us go back to Judea." - John 11:1-7, NIV

Lazarus, Mary, and Martha were three siblings who were close friends of Jesus. He would stay with them when He was in town. They financially supported His ministry. They were people Jesus could always count on to be there for Him when He had a need, and they felt the same, because, when Lazarus was sick, the sisters sent for Jesus to help.

Two days after receiving the news that Lazarus was sick, Jesus rallied the boys and said He wanted to go back to Judea. His disciples weren't really thrilled with this decision.

"But Rabbi," they said, "a short while ago the Jews there
tried to stone you, and yet you are going back?" - John 11:8,
NIV

They were stunned that He wanted to go back. It was true. The Jews in Judea had just tried to stone Him, and now He was going to risk it all and go back? Why take the chance? Why put His life in danger? How did Jesus respond?

Jesus answered, "Are there not twelve hours of daylight?
Anyone who walks in the daytime will not stumble, for they
see by this world's light. It is when a person walks at night
that they stumble, for they have no light."

After he had said this, he went on to tell them, "Our friend
Lazarus has fallen asleep; but I am going there to wake him
up." - John 11:9-11, NIV

What did Jesus mean by all of that about the daytime and daylight? Don't feel bad if this confused you. I was confused by it, too. So I looked this passage up in a few commentaries, and basically, Jesus was saying that He had an appointed time to live and minister and an appointed time to die. The dying time was coming soon, but it wasn't there yet. He then went on to say that Lazarus was asleep and He had to wake him up. By sleeping, He meant dead.

Yes, it is a confusing way to say Lazarus was dead, and it apparently confused the disciples as well.

> *His disciples replied, "Lord, if he sleeps, he will get better." Jesus had been speaking of his death, but his disciples thought he meant natural sleep.*
>
> *So then he told them plainly, "Lazarus is dead, and for your sake I am glad I was not there, so that you may believe. But let us go to him." - John 11:12-14, NIV*

Jesus makes it clear, Lazarus was dead, but there was still something He could do about it. He knew this was an opportunity to increase His disciples' faith and get more glory for His Father. If you read the remainder of Luke 11, you will see that Jesus went to Bethany and brought Lazarus back to life! It was one of Jesus' greatest miracles. But this chapter isn't about Lazarus, it is about Thomas, so I don't want to focus on that part of the story. Instead, I want to look at the verse I skipped, verse 16.

In the next verse, we see Thomas' response to Jesus' decision to go to Bethany. He knew Jesus had just escaped an assassination attempt the last time they were there. He heard Jesus say that His time to die hadn't arrived yet, but it was coming. Thomas' pessimistic, worst-case-scenario outlook heard this, and he realized that bad things were coming down the road. But when we read the following verse, we see something glorious!

> *Then Thomas (also known as Didymus) said to the rest of the disciples, "Let us also go, that we may die with him." - John 11:16, NIV*

"Jamie, what's so great about that? He is such a Debbie-Downer, saying, 'We're all going to die'".

That is not what I see in this passage. What I see is a man who takes action to overcome his bad personality trait and says, *"We're probably gonna die, but I will ride or die with Jesus anyway!"*

This statement by Thomas, while being stated in a negative form which is very much his personality, shows him overcoming that personality to follow Jesus. He naturally wouldn't have a ride or die attitude, but he had allowed time with Jesus to change who he was, and now he could make decisions and take actions that were counter to his natural disposition.

I think this is huge for all of us. We all tend to let our personalities and comfort levels dictate what we will and will not do. We don't tend to naturally do uncomfortable things. But there are no such things as comfort zones in God's kingdom. There is just obedience and following, no highway option.

Being a ride or die follower of God doesn't come naturally to anyone, but, let's be honest, it is even harder for some of us than others. Trust issues, situations from our past, fears, failures, personality tendencies, so many things cause some to really struggle with this level of surrender and devotion.

In our family, I tend to be a little more adventurous and bold. This carries over into my riding or dying with God. Adessa tends to be a little more cautious and realistic. She worries and stresses more about things. Whenever God calls us to a new level of ride or die, I am usually faster to jump than she is. It's just our personalities. It takes her a little longer to make the leap. But she always overcomes her natural tendency and chooses that, even though it makes her uncomfortable and scared, she will trust God and ride and die with Him. Let me give you some examples of what I mean.

When God gave me the vision to start Mantour Ministries and the conferences, this was a HUGE ride or die decision. It took everything we had to do it, financially, spiritually, and faith-wise. I was the first of the two of us to jump feet first into this new venture. Being more realistic and cautious, Adessa laid down the parameters we could do. She said we could do four conferences. That was all the finances we could afford. If they failed and no one came, we would lose everything but not go into debt doing it. She committed to ride or die in her own way and how she felt comfortable, but she did ride or die! We ended up doing seven conferences that year. As God opened doors, she rallied her courage and said, *"Let's do this,"* knowing there was a good possibility we'd end up broke. Thankfully, we did not.

Here is another example. Recently, God began to speak to me that He wanted us to buy a new (used) vehicle. At the time, this made no sense. We had a Toyota Rav4 with 100,000 miles, and we figured it would last another 100,000 miles. But we were struggling to fit everything into this SUV because of the mobility scooter I use.

Because of the stimulus checks and a little savings, we could barely afford to do this. In my mind, God said it, we take the leap and go all in, even if it meant completely draining all of our savings. Adessa, being the more plan-ahead type-A personality, struggled more than I did to do it. In her mind, we had a car that ran well, and God couldn't really be telling me to do this.

However, God wouldn't let it go, and He started telling her what He was telling me. While it was a way tougher decision for her to obey God and trust Him to do what He was asking, she chose to go ahead and ride or die with Him, even if it cost all our financial savings and security.

We ended up buying a used minivan. (Choosing this vehicle was way harder for me than her. In this case, I was the one who had to surrender and ride or die with what God wanted.) Weeks later, the mobility scooter I use died, and I had to get a new one. God miraculously supplied the money for this purchase, but because of the chip shortage around the world and the cargo shipping issues we were experiencing as a country, I couldn't find a new scooter anywhere. They were all on backorder for months!

I called almost every scooter store in a five-state radius and checked every website I could with no luck. I FINALLY found one store hours away that had a scooter. However, this scooter was bigger and heavier than my old one, and I couldn't lift it myself. So we had to get a scooter lift installed in our van. Again, God miraculously supplied the funds for this purchase! All of a sudden, it became crystal clear why God had told us to get a bigger vehicle! There was no way a scooter and a lift would fit inside of our Rav4, not to mention the boxes of books and suitcases we need to minister.

It was really tough for Adessa to commit our entire savings and buy a new (used) van, but she overcame her struggle and chose to ride or die with God because He asked. I admire her for this. Honestly, she exhibits a greater trust in God because it is so against her personality. But she always chooses to ride or die.

Thomas was like this. It was harder for him than it would be for a guy like Peter *"The Rock,"* James and John the *"Sons of Thunder,"* or Simon *"The Zealot."* But Thomas did trust Jesus completely. We know this because his personality should have made him the last one to begin the trek back to Judea. But he overcame his natural disposition, and he boldly claimed, *"Guys, let's go! Even if we die doing it, I am riding or dying with Jesus."*

Thomas shows us that our personality, our past, our trust issues, NOTHING can keep us from truly riding or dying with Jesus. We have the power to overcome and walk in faith, believing we must do it because Jesus called us to do it. No matter what it is, you can overcome it.

- Maybe you struggle to share your faith with others because you're shy or timid.

- Maybe it's hard to trust God to come through because you have faced disappointments in the past.

- Maybe you struggle to trust God to be there with you because people have abandoned you.

- Maybe it's hard to surrender because you have been burned by decisions in the past.

- Maybe you can't take a financial leap because you grew up poor or struggling financially.

The same power that raised Jesus from the dead lives in you and this power can help you overcome your natural tendencies or struggles.

- Maybe you struggle to take risks because you have experienced failure.

There are so many reasons people struggle to boldly lay down everything to ride or die with God. I get that. I have experienced that. It can be hard. But it can be done!

You can overcome! You can gain victory. You can trust God to always ride or die with you when you ride or die with Him. The same power that raised Jesus from the dead lives in you, and this power can help you overcome your natural tendencies or struggles.

How do you do it? Spend time in prayer with God and share with Him your fears and struggles. Tell Him it is hard for you to ride or die with Him, but you want to do it anyway. Ask Him for a supernatural boldness to replace your natural hesitance. Then commit to ride or die with Him no matter what. Then, when push comes to shove, make a choice to surrender, no matter how hard it is, and ride or die. Even if it comes out a little negative like it did with Thomas, push through and do it.

I believe in you! There is no struggle, tendency, personality trait, fear, or issue that God's power can't overcome. Your personality doesn't have to define you. Jesus can redefine you. Choose to ride and die with Him, no matter what comes naturally.

Group Study Questions:

1. Did you have a nickname growing up? Was it a positive or negative nickname? How did it affect you?

2. Thomas shows us it is possible to overcome our personalities and boldly follow Jesus. What area of your life or personality keeps you from riding or dying with God?

3. This chapter states: *"There are no such things as comfort zones in God's kingdom. There is just obedience and following, no highway option."* How does this statement make you feel?

4. What area of your life do you feel the most timid?

5. How can you overcome this timidity and move forward with a ride or die attitude?

6. After reading this chapter, what is one thing you will put into practice or one thing you will change in your life?

7. How can we, as a group, help you do this?

CHAPTER FOUR

RIDE OR DIE WHOLEHEARTEDLY

Then Peter spoke up, "We have left everything to follow you!"

Thank you for reading this book. I love it when a man of God invests time to grow spiritually!

When I was a kid, I LOVED to read. I would read for hours. Every year at Christmas, I would get at least one book for Christmas, and it barely made it through December 26 before I had read it cover to cover. I really enjoyed a good story. Maybe that is why I am drawn to using stories of men in the Bible as the basis of my books.

Anyway, my love for reading hasn't really faded, but I don't read nearly as much as I did in my past. Whenever I buy a new book now, I get the Kindle version. We are out of bookshelf space! But I still have many of my favorite old books.

One Christmas, about 20 years ago, I received a book from my mom and dad. It was by one of my heroes of the faith, Fred Stoeker. The book was called *"Every Man's Challenge."* (Great book, you should read it!) The subtitle of the book posed an interesting question. *"How far are you willing to go for God?"*

That is a great question. It is a question that all men need to face. It is basically asking, *"Will you ride or die for God?"* I want to examine this a little further in this chapter by looking at the lives of two different men. Both of these men had the opportunity to ride or die right next to Jesus. They each had the great opportunity of serving and learning side by side with Jesus. Unfortunately, because of his divided heart, one ended up sad, alone, and apart from God. The other chose to ride or die with Jesus and has become a living legend. Their stories clearly warn against allowing things to stand between us riding and dying with God.

Most people familiar with the four Gospels know that John was often known as *"the disciple who Jesus loved."* However, in the Gospel of Luke, we see that this title was almost stolen by another man who came seeking out Jesus. To see his story, let's look at Luke 18.

> **A certain ruler asked him, "Good teacher, what must I do to inherit eternal life?" - Luke 18:18, NIV**

In Luke, we read this man was a ruler. In other Gospel accounts, we read that he was a younger man. Being a ruler meant he was a leader of the local synagogue. He would have been a well-respected, influential, righteous man who many people knew. This is what makes it so odd that he came to Jesus asking this question.

First of all, the rulers weren't really Jesus' biggest fans. They kind of hated His guts!

Second, to the average onlooker, it seemed he was the model of the man who deserved eternal life. If there were a *Who's Who of*

Eternal Life, most would assume this guy's name would be towards the top of the list.

Many observing this scene probably wondered if he was just another leader trying to make a name for himself by questioning Jesus. He certainly wasn't the first person to throw a theology question at Jesus, trying to expose Him as less than holy. However, as we read on, we see that Jesus didn't look suspiciously at the man. He didn't throw a "*Woe*" at him as He often did to rulers and Pharisees. Instead, He looked him in the eye and sincerely answered the question.

> *"Why do you call me good?" Jesus answered. "No one is good—except God alone. You know the commandments: 'You shall not commit adultery, you shall not murder, you shall not steal, you shall not give false testimony, honor your father and mother.'" - Luke 18:19-20, NIV*

Jesus, knowing this young man thought a lot of himself, tried to direct his attention to the fact that no human could be labeled "*good.*" All men are sinners. Only God is truly good. If Jesus wouldn't take this praise for Himself as God's Son, then this man definitely had no right to think this way about himself.

Jesus instead reminds the man that the only way to be labeled "*good*" is to totally and completely obey the Law of Moses. Since this is impossible, the only conclusion to be reached is that no one can do anything to obtain salvation. It can only come through the one good person, God. As we read on, we see that the young ruler totally misses Jesus' point.

> *"All these I have kept since I was a boy," he said. - Luke 18:21, NIV*

Wow! How's that for an arrogant statement! In essence, he is saying he has never done anything wrong. He felt he lived a genuinely holy life. Spiritually, he thought he was the man! He did the deeds, said the prayers, made the required sacrifices. He had arrived spiritually, onto eternal life!

This young man had a wrong view of salvation and righteousness. He felt it came from obeying a list of rules and regulations. He failed to recognize that salvation and eternal life only come through admitting our needs, turning to God for the forgiveness of our sins, and devoting our lives to ride or die as God's servant. He had a lot to learn, and Jesus was about to take him to school.

Let's switch to Mark's Gospel now. Remember, Peter mentored Mark, and he wrote his Gospel based on Peter's first-hand observations. In Mark's account, we see something that only someone there could notice. Let's look at Mark 10.

Jesus looked at him and loved him.... - Mark 10:21, NIV

What an awesome statement. Jesus loved this young man. He saw great potential for this young ruler's life and ministry. He saw inside of this man an earnest desire to learn the truth. Jesus wanted this young man to be one of His disciples. However, He had to see if the young man was serious about following Him or not. He poses an interesting situation to the young man.

> ***Jesus looked at him and loved him. "One thing you lack," he said. "Go, sell everything you have and give to the poor, and you will have treasure in heaven. Then come, follow me." - Mark 10:21, NIV***

Basically, Jesus is calling this young man to ride or die with Him. He is issuing a challenge for this young man to lay aside everything else in his life and serve Jesus wholeheartedly. Unfortunately, the young man's heart was divided.

At this the man's face fell. He went away sad, because he had great wealth. - Mark 10:22, NIV

On the one hand, he wanted to serve God and live the life of a disciple, yet he also wanted to hang onto his usual, familiar way of life. For this man, his normal life was a rich, luxurious lifestyle. However, the money isn't the issue here. Money is never the issue. The real issue is the heart of the man.

He wanted to serve God the way he wanted to do it. He wanted to stay comfortable. He didn't want to change his ways. He wanted some of God, but he didn't want to ride or die all the way, giving His 100% loyalty to Jesus.

Most of all, he didn't want to surrender everything to God. He would go part way, but he held back. Complete, unconditional surrender was not an option. He wanted Jesus, but he also wanted what he knew and what made him comfortable. He didn't want to sacrifice anything to follow Jesus.

Jesus asked him to go too far, further than he was willing. As a result, he left sad, hopeless, and alone. He had a chance to have the ultimate experience serving side-by-side with Jesus, being remembered throughout history as the thirteenth disciple, but his heart was divided. He couldn't bring himself to ride or die with Jesus. Guys, we must make sure we don't make the same mistake.

You may be thinking, *"Jamie, not a problem for me. I don't have a lot of money, so it won't come between God and me."*

Money is not the issue we are discussing. Most of us have never been in a position of great wealth. However, we all have things in our lives that, left unchecked, can keep our hearts divided from fully following God. What if God approached you and asked these things of you?

- What if God asked you to give up your fifteen minutes in the morning reading Facebook and replace it with Bible reading?

- What if God asked you to give up your favorite tv show because it promoted magic and witchcraft?

- How about if God asked you to stop hanging out with some friends because they are causing you to compromise too much?

- If God asked you not to play Fantasy Football for a season and instead volunteer to lead a group of teens at your church, would you give it up?

- If you were offered the job of your dreams that you had been working so hard to achieve, would you turn it down because God wants you to spend more time with both Him and your family?

To reach our full potential as God's man, we must be willing to hold nothing back.

Deciding to really commit to ride or die with God is an issue we all must face. To reach our full potential as God's man, we must be willing to hold nothing back.

This is a decision I have had to face in my life. Even recently, I experienced some major upheaval in my life, and I did NOT like what was going on. I wanted OUT! I wanted to run. The urge to quit was never so strong in my life. But God said to me, *"Jamie, will you stay with Me on this? Will you sacrifice your desires, your wishes, your will and simply ride or die through this hard time?"* I had to choose to ride or die through these horrible circumstances.

This is just a small example of the many ways God tests us to see if we have a divided heart. I have had to give up dreams, aspirations, relationships, thought patterns, and even the image I tried to present to people to follow God wholeheartedly. He hasn't let me keep anything that keeps me from wholeheartedly following Him. For this, I am thankful. While it hurts to cut out the things that cause a divided heart, it in no way equals the pain and disappointment that we endure when we realize that we could have had more with God.

The rich young ruler shows us the grief of allowing our hearts to stay divided. We must choose to surrender everything to God. Need someone to look to for inspiration to ride or die wholeheartedly?

A great example of a man who, unlike the young ruler, did give it all up to follow Jesus was Peter. Peter left his life as a fisherman, his security, everything he had, to follow Jesus.

After the rich young ruler walked away from Jesus, Jesus began to teach about how hard it is for anyone to follow Him. Few will pay the price, as demonstrated by this young ruler. However, not all refuse to pay it. Many are willing to follow Jesus wholeheartedly. Peter was one of them. Let's look at Mark 10 again:

> *Then Peter spoke up, "We have left everything to follow you!"*
>
> *"Truly I tell you," Jesus replied, "no one who has left home or brothers or sisters or mother or father or children or fields for me and the gospel will fail to receive a hundred times as much in this present age: homes, brothers, sisters, mothers, children and fields—along with persecutions— and in the age to come eternal life." - Mark 10:28-30, NIV*

In another passage, we again see Peter having to decide if He will ride or die with Jesus. In John 6, we read that Jesus taught some challenging, unpopular teachings, and the crowds who followed Him didn't want to hear it. Many of His followers abandoned Jesus because they felt His call to ride or die was too costly, too demanding. At this moment, Jesus said to his twelve disciples:

"Do you also want to leave?" - John 6:67, MSG

Jesus was once again asking His disciples, *"Are you sure you still want to ride or die with Me?"*

How did Peter answer?

Peter replied, "Master, to whom would we go? You have the words of real life, eternal life. We've already committed ourselves, confident that you are the Holy One of God." - John 6:68-69, MSG

Peter was 100% committed to ride or die with Jesus! To him, there was no going back. It was a 100% ride or die commitment to walk with Jesus, no matter what!

What a stark contrast there is between these two men. One was a fan of Jesus, and the other was 100% committed, sold out, and riding or dying with Him wholeheartedly. Jesus' final words to Peter and the rich young ruler that we read earlier still ring true today. The rich young ruler and his divided heart died, and along with him, all of his wealth. Peter, on the other hand, went 100% in with Jesus, leaving everything behind.

Two thousand years later, Peter lives in infamy. He wrote two books of the Bible and also is responsible for telling Mark the contents of the Gospel of Mark. Many lives have been changed through Peter's life. The same can't be said of the ruler with a divided heart.

This is such an important topic. Nothing can keep us from riding or dying more than having a divided heart. Too many of God's sons are letting distractions keep them from following God with reckless abandon. They want to follow God and serve Him, but on their terms, not His. They want the blessing of God without the wholehearted commitment to Him. They don't want to do without anything.

In many cases, they want what the world has. They want to go to the places the world goes. They want to watch the things the world watches. They want to drink what the world drinks and entertain what the world entertains.

To ride or die, we have to do it with all we have. Distractions can't get in the way. Compromise can't keep us chasing the ways of the world. We have to follow God wholeheartedly and give up the things God asks us to surrender to Him.

This chapter shows two distinct paths. On one path was a man who wasn't all in with God and wouldn't give up the things God asked him to surrender. He wouldn't sacrifice the temporal things of earth to ride and die with the King of eternity. On the other hand was a man who gave up everything to follow God. He held nothing back! One is looked at as a failure in history, and one is a living legend, the rock that God used to build His church!

Which example will you follow? You need to take a hard look at your life.

Is there sin which you are holding on to that God wants you to give up for Him??

Is there something that you are holding onto, something that you won't surrender to God?

Will you surrender it to God?

What are you willing to give up for God?

What are you willing to separate yourself from for Him?

How far will you go for God?

Will you ride or die with Him with your whole heart, soul, mind, and being, holding nothing back?

Maybe you have never accepted Christ into your heart. He is waiting now for you to come to Him. Or perhaps you are a Christian who just hasn't surrendered to God. You want all of God that you can have, but you are holding onto that one sin, that one action, that one relationship.

Please, right now, surrender your life to God. Surrender your will. Follow God wholeheartedly. Only then can you have God's presence in a way that you never thought possible. Only then can you experience victory. Only then can you ride or die with God!

Group Study Questions:

1. The rich young ruler had the wrong idea of what it takes to follow God. How would you define what it takes to follow God?

2. The rich young ruler wouldn't surrender everything to God. Is there anything that you struggle to submit that is keeping you from riding or dying with God?

3. Why do you think Peter could surrender and follow God wholeheartedly, but the rich young ruler couldn't?

4. What are you willing to give up for God?

5. What are you willing to separate yourself from for Him?

6. Will you ride or die with Him with your whole heart, soul, mind, and being, holding nothing back?

7. After reading this chapter, what is one thing you will put into practice or one thing you will change in your life?

8. How can we, as a group, help you do this?

CHAPTER FIVE

RIDE OR DIE WITH PURPOSE

"I am carrying on a great project and cannot go down. Why should the work stop while I leave it and go down to you?"

I LOVE a great project, something to sink my teeth into, something that gives me a sense of purpose. Whether it be a construction project, a ministry project, or a personal goal to work towards, I thrive best when I have a sense of purpose.

I think most men are this way. One of the saddest things I see happening across the world today is that too many men are living their lives without a sense of purpose. They are just going through the motions with work, family, church, filling their time with hobbies, but not having a true sense of purpose.

This is not how God created His men to live. We are not meant to get through life, just filling time and waiting for something exciting to come along. I believe that God created every one of us with a specific purpose in mind. Our job is to figure out what that purpose is and then to spend our lives riding and dying to fulfill that purpose.

Finding your purpose doesn't necessarily mean a full-time call to ministry. I am talking about finding your purpose, the one thing God created you to do. In this chapter, we are going to look at the life of a man who found his purpose and pursued it with every ounce of strength he had. Let's look at the life of Nehemiah.

> *The words of Nehemiah son of Hakaliah: In the month of Kislev in the twentieth year, while I was in the citadel of Susa, Hanani, one of my brothers, came from Judah with some other men, and I questioned them about the Jewish remnant that had survived the exile, and also about Jerusalem.*
>
> *They said to me, "Those who survived the exile and are back in the province are in great trouble and disgrace. The wall of Jerusalem is broken down, and its gates have been burned with fire." - Nehemiah 1:1-3, NIV*

Nehemiah was one of the Israelites who lived in exile after God judged Israel for their deplorable sins. He was probably born in exile, away from his homeland and his people. Even though he lived in Susa, his heart was with his people in Israel.

When he heard this news from his brother about how his fellow Jewish people suffered back home, it broke him. He was heartbroken to hear how the city was in ruins, and the wall was destroyed, leaving his fellow brethren open and exposed to looting and attack. He longed to make things right. At this moment, he found his purpose, the reason he was born, the thing he was called to do.

Nehemiah dropped to his knees and prayed this prayer.

"God, God-of-Heaven, the great and awesome God, loyal to his covenant and faithful to those who love him and obey his commands: Look at me, listen to me. Pay attention to this prayer of your servant that I'm praying day and night in intercession for your servants, the People of Israel, confessing the sins of the People of Israel. And I'm including myself, I and my ancestors, among those who have sinned against you.

We've treated you like dirt: We haven't done what you told us, haven't followed your commands, and haven't respected the decisions you gave to Moses your servant. All the same, remember the warning you posted to your servant Moses: 'If you betray me, I'll scatter you to the four winds, but if you come back to me and do what I tell you, I'll gather up all these scattered peoples from wherever they ended up and put them back in the place I chose to mark with my Name.'

Well, there they are—your servants, your people whom you so powerfully and impressively redeemed. O Master, listen to me, listen to your servant's prayer—and yes, to all your servants who delight in honoring you—and make me successful today so that I get what I want from the king." - *Nehemiah 1:5-11, MSG*

Nehemiah begged God to forgive the nation of Israel, restore the city and people, and use him to do it. He asked God to give him favor before the king to make the request. But how was this poor exile ever going to get the chance to even approach the king? That brings us to our first point.

1. Your purpose is to do what only you can do.

I love the last verse of this chapter:

I was cupbearer to the king. - *Nehemiah 1:11, MSG*

Way to bury the lead! He worked for the king! He had one of the most important jobs in the kingdom! He was the king's cupbearer. This meant he brought the king his food and his wine. Big deal, right? It was a big deal! Being the king's cupbearer was a sweet gig, and only someone the king trusted implicitly could hold this position.

Kings in this time were constantly worried about treason or being overthrown. The king had to trust the guy bringing him his food and beverages. The cupbearer had to have a good relationship with the king so the king knew that he would never slip a little something-something into the food or drink to kill him.

Personally, if I was Nehemiah, I would have said in verse one, *"I'm Nehemiah, the king's cupbearer. I work at the palace. Me and the king are tight. We talk all the time."* But he didn't. He doesn't even mention it until it was absolutely necessary. That's because Nehemiah didn't get his purpose from his career. He got it from his identity as a child of God. His true purpose wasn't yucking it up with the king. It was helping the hurting people back home.

After Nehemiah prayed, he went to work to do his job, but his heart and mind were back home with his people. Still, he waited for God to open the door for him to speak to the king. Four months later, he got his chance.

> **In the month of Nisan in the twentieth year of King Artaxerxes, when wine was brought for him, I took the wine and gave it to the king. I had not been sad in his presence before, so the king asked me, "Why does your face look so sad when you are not ill? This can be nothing but sadness of heart." - Nehemiah 2:1-2, NIV**

Four months after hearing about the news back home, Nehemiah was still sad and shaken up about it. Even though he daily lived in the luxury of the palace working with the king, his heart and mind were back with his people. He had a new burning purpose, to help his people. But he had to wait for God's timing.

> *I was very much afraid, but I said to the king, "May the king live forever! Why should my face not look sad when the city where my ancestors are buried lies in ruins, and its gates have been destroyed by fire?"*
>
> *The king said to me, "What is it you want?"*
>
> *Then I prayed to the God of heaven, and I answered the king, "If it pleases the king and if your servant has found favor in his sight, let him send me to the city in Judah where my ancestors are buried so that I can rebuild it." - Nehemiah 2:2-5, NIV*

Shaking from fear but emboldened by his newfound purpose, Nehemiah knew this was the moment. He told the king what was going on back home and asked the king to let him go back to fix the wall and rebuild the city so his people could be safe and protected. Because of his access to the king, he was able to speak about his purpose with the king. This was the one job only Nehemiah could do.

Your purpose isn't always a call to full-time ministry, but it's always to do something with your talents and abilities that need to be done to further God's kingdom.

Nehemiah found favor from the king. The king commissioned him to rebuild the city and the wall. The king even gave him letters of authority, the materials to build the wall, and a protection detail of officers and calvary to protect him.

Nehemiah had a new sense of purpose, and he decided he would ride or die with God to fulfill that purpose. Notice, he didn't go back to his people as a priest, a preacher, or a rabbi. He went as a construction foreman to do manual work. Your purpose isn't always a call to full-time ministry, but it's always to do something with your talents and abilities that need to be done to further God's kingdom.

So Nehemiah went back to his homeland, rebuilt the wall, easy-peasy-lemon-squeezy, right?

Wrong. This brings us to point two.

2. We must stand strong in our purpose even when we face resistance.

Almost immediately, Nehemiah faced obstacles standing in his way.

> *When Sanballat the Horonite and Tobiah the Ammonite official heard about this, they were very much disturbed that someone had come to promote the welfare of the Israelites. - Nehemiah 2:10, NIV*

Of course, they didn't like this news. Up until now, the Ammonites could loot, pillage, and persecute these unprotected Israelites. Now someone was coming to put an end to it. They decided to put an end to Nehemiah and his purpose.

Nehemiah arrived and immediately rallied his fellow Israelites with a rousing speech about why they should rebuild the wall and the city. The people rallied around Nehemiah's vision and started rebuilding the wall. This didn't go over well with Tobiah and Sanballat.

> *When Sanballat heard that we were rebuilding the wall, he became angry and was greatly incensed. He ridiculed the*

Jews, and in the presence of his associates and the army of Samaria, he said, "What are those feeble Jews doing? Will they restore their wall? Will they offer sacrifices? Will they finish in a day? Can they bring the stones back to life from those heaps of rubble—burned as they are?"

Tobiah the Ammonite, who was at his side, said, "What they are building—even a fox climbing up on it would break down their wall of stones!" - Nehemiah 4:1-3, NIV

Let me be honest with you. When you make the decision to ride or die with purpose, people are going to make fun of you. Don't believe me? Take an hour and look at social media, especially Twitter, and see how people talk about Christians who are doing their best to walk in their calling and purpose. It is BRUTAL. The world will mock you, try to intimidate you, and discourage you. Even fellow believers may try and do it...but you need to ride or die anyway!

I remember nine years ago when God gave me my purpose, to start Mantour Conferences to reach men. I had a pastor tell me my ministry was worthless. Another asked why I thought I could do it since I didn't grow up in a family of pastors and wasn't well known in my denomination. I had more than one person tell me not to bother, men wouldn't be interested, I'd probably only get maybe 100 guys to turn out, and that small of a turnout wasn't worth all the effort. I had to ignore these negative attitudes and do what I felt was my God-given purpose. Even if only ten men showed up, I would or ride or die with God!

Nehemiah knew what he was called to do, he knew his purpose, and he went on with the work. As a result, he faced a new level of obstacle...persecution.

So we rebuilt the wall till all of it reached half its height, for the people worked with all their heart.

But when Sanballat, Tobiah, the Arabs, the Ammonites and the people of Ashdod heard that the repairs to Jerusalem's walls had gone ahead and that the gaps were being closed, they were very angry. They all plotted together to come and fight against Jerusalem and stir up trouble against it. -Nehemiah 4:6-8, NIV

Nehemiah and the people no longer faced just taunting. Now they faced physical persecution. How did they respond?

But we prayed to our God and posted a guard day and night to meet this threat. - Nehemiah 6:9, NIV

When persecution and resistance to your purpose come against you, you need to follow Nehemiah's example, drop to your knees, ask God for strength and victory, and continue to do the mission.

Nehemiah dropped to his knees, asked God for help and protection, and then continued the work. Not even the threat of physical violence kept him from riding or dying with purpose.

When persecution and resistance to your purpose come against you, you need to follow Nehemiah's example, drop to your knees, ask God for strength and victory, and continue to do the mission.

Meanwhile, the people in Judah said, "The strength of the laborers is giving out, and there is so much rubble that we cannot rebuild the wall."

Also our enemies said, "Before they know it or see us, we will be right there among them and will kill them and put an end to the work."

Then the Jews who lived near them came and told us ten times over, "Wherever you turn, they will attack us."

Therefore I stationed some of the people behind the lowest points of the wall at the exposed places, posting them by families, with their swords, spears and bows. After I looked things over, I stood up and said to the nobles, the officials and the rest of the people, "Don't be afraid of them. Remember the Lord, who is great and awesome, and fight for your families, your sons and your daughters, your wives and your homes."

When our enemies heard that we were aware of their plot and that God had frustrated it, we all returned to the wall, each to our own work. - Nehemiah 4:10-15, NIV

Even when his own workforce began to falter, Nehemiah did whatever he had to do to make sure the job got done. He made sure he achieved his goal. He knew his purpose, he made sure they did whatever was necessary to finish the job, and he and the people eventually rebuilt the wall.

Once the wall was finished, Nehemiah was able to take a victory lap around the city before heading back to be the king's cupbearer, right? Wrong!

When word came to Sanballat, Tobiah, Geshem the Arab and the rest of our enemies that I had rebuilt the wall and not a gap was left in it—though up to that time I had not set the doors in the gates— Sanballat and Geshem sent me this message: "Come, let us meet together in one of the villages on the plain of Ono."

But they were scheming to harm me... - Nehemiah 6:1-2, NIV

Under a guise of a peace meeting, the enemies of Nehemiah tried to take one last shot at him. Before he could get the gates installed, shutting them out completely, they tried to stop him. How did he respond?

> *I sent messengers to them with this reply: "I am carrying on a great project and cannot go down. Why should the work stop while I leave it and go down to you?" Four times they sent me the same message, and each time I gave them the same answer. - Nehemiah 6:3-4, NIV*

I LOVE THIS REPLY! Nehemiah was riding or dying with purpose. He knew his purpose was too important to stop doing it for a meeting with the enemy. Instead of entertaining the enemy's discouragement, persecution, and attempts to end his mission, he simply said what he was doing was too important. He couldn't come down. Four different times, he had to take this stance. This brings us to our third point.

3. Always keep your eyes on the mission.

Nehemiah always had both eyes on his purpose, setting up his people with safety and security. He had a building project that needed to be completed. His people's very lives depended on it. It wasn't about him; it was about them.

Your purpose is important. What you do and how well you do it will affect more than you. It will affect others around you. You have no idea what eternal consequences your work will have on the life of another person.

Recently, I received a call from a pastor telling me a story. He was counseling a young man who was struggling with addiction and suicidal thoughts. He was new to the church and a new believer. At the end of the session, the pastor gave this man a copy of my book, *"Invincible."* The pastor said this young man devoured the book, and as a result, he became a different man. It was a life-changing thing for this young man, something about what he read helped him work through and gain victory. The pastor was calling me to encourage me to keep doing what I was doing and to thank me for walking in my purpose.

If I had let the discouraging words of others I mentioned earlier stop me from walking in my purpose, it could have had a huge effect on this man's life. I don't say that arrogantly or with an *"ain't I great attitude."* I say it humbly to make the point that you do not know what eternal consequences your ride or die decision to fulfill your God-given purpose will have on others.

Nehemiah knew his work was too important. He refused to come down. The work was too great! He chose to ride or die with purpose, and he finished the job!

So the wall was completed on the twenty-fifth of Elul, in fifty-two days. - Nehemiah 6:15, NIV

The wall was complete, the city was safe, and his people were secure. Mission accomplished. All because he knew the work was too great and he couldn't come down.

Every time I read this passage, I think about another man in the Bible. This man was born for one purpose and one purpose only. He knew what His purpose was, and He chose to ride or die to fulfill His purpose. This man was Jesus.

Jesus was born to be the needed sacrifice for man's sins. He was born to live and die for every one of us. The only way we could be reunited with God was for Jesus to take on humanity to die for our sins. He was the only One Who could do it. He faced mocking, ridicule, and even persecution as He walked the earth, but He chose to ride or die with His Father's purpose. Even when in the garden of Gethsemane, He said to His Father, *"Not My will, but Your will be done."* He was basically saying, *"Father, is there any chance I don't have to do this…but if I must, I will ride or die with You and the purpose You have given to Me."*

Jesus went to the cross to fulfill His purpose. Even on the cross, beaten and abused, He faced the temptation to give up on His purpose. *"Come down from the cross if you're all you claim to be,"* they mocked and jeered. (Matthew 27:40)

Jesus could have come right off of that cross. He had the power to send an army of angels to silence His enemies. But with a ride or die sense of purpose, He ignored their taunts. His work was too great; He couldn't come down!

Your work, your purpose, the one thing God created you to do is too important for you to not do it. You cannot come down!

You must choose, like Nehemiah and Jesus, to commit yourself to discover what your true purpose is in life. Then you must choose to give it all you got. No matter what obstacles you face or what comes against you, you must ride or die with purpose.

Your work is too great. Only you can do it. You cannot stop. Embrace your purpose and pursue it with all of your passion! Give it all you got. Then see what God can do!

Group Study Questions:

1. What does it mean to find your purpose?

2. How do we respond when we face resistance from the enemy and others as we pursue our purpose?

3. In this chapter, we stated, *"You do not know what eternal consequences your ride or die decision to fulfill your God-given purpose will have on others."* What does this mean? How does it challenge you to fulfill your purpose?

4. What is the biggest obstacle keeping you from fulfilling your purpose?

5. What can you do to overcome this obstacle?

6. After reading this chapter, what is one thing you will put into practice or one thing you will change in your life?

7. How can we, as a group, help you do this?

CHAPTER SIX

RIDE OR DIE FOR GOD, NOT HIS BLESSINGS

God said [to Abraham], "Take your son, your only son, whom you love—
Isaac—and go to the region of Moriah. Sacrifice him there as a burnt
offering on a mountain I will show you."

The other day I was looking at my Facebook feed when I saw an interesting post. It said, *"Would you streak through a shopping mall for two minutes for $75 million?"*

I have to admit I didn't have to think long at all before I answered to myself, *"Of course!"* That is a lot of money, I don't embarrass easily, and I could live worry-free doing what God called me to do for the rest of my life. Even after the government takes their 50%, and you pay the legal fees when they catch you, you'd still probably have at least $30-35 million left. Sign me up!

I have seen many similar posts on social media.

- *Would you live in this mountain top cabin without your cell phone for a year if you got to keep it afterward?*

- *Would you give up the internet for this beachside mansion?*

- *Would you live on a deserted island with your 5th @ if you won a million dollars in the end?*

I've seen many of these posts over the years on social media. However, I have never seen one that said, *"Would you run naked through a mall for two minutes for $75 million, but you have to give it all back in two years?"*

Only a true nudist would even consider this! It wouldn't be worth it if you only get to hold the money for a period of time but never spend it. Why humiliate yourself to hold someone else's money for a few months?

Do we ride or die for God because of what we can get out of it, or do we do it simply because He asks us to?

The fact of the matter is, we would only consider such embarrassment or hardships to get something out of it ourselves.

I wonder how often we make the same decision in our spiritual lives? Do we ride or die for God because of what we can get out of it, or do we do it simply because He asks us to? In this chapter, we will examine the life of a man who faced this dilemma. Let's check out Abraham's story.

We first read about Abraham in Genesis 12, where he is going by his old name of Abram.

> *The Lord had said to Abram, "Go from your country, your people and your father's household to the land I will show you.   I will make you into a great nation, and I will bless you; I will make your name great, and you will be a blessing.   I will bless those who bless you, and whoever curses you I will curse;   and all peoples on earth will be blessed through you." - Genesis 12:1-3, NIV*

How's that for a sweet deal! Imagine logging onto Facebook and seeing a post that said, *"Would you move out of your house into a new home, taking all your possessions with you, if you got to finally have an heir that you longed for your entire life and has alluded you for 75 years, and have this heir be the leader of My Kingdom? Oh, and you also will be eternally blessed, and no one can ever harm you?"*

Where is my nearest U-haul station…sign me up!

Abraham had the same reaction because we continue to read:

> *So Abram went, as the Lord had told him…. Abram was seventy-five years old when he set out from Harran.   He took his wife Sarai, his nephew Lot, all the possessions they had accumulated and the people they had acquired in Harran, and they set out for the land of Canaan, and they arrived there.*
>
> *Abram traveled through the land as far as the site of the great tree of Moreh at Shechem. At that time the Canaanites were in the land. The Lord appeared to Abram and said, "To your offspring I will give this land." So he built an altar there to the Lord, who had appeared to him. - Genesis 12:4-7, NIV*

God had made a deal with Abraham. *"If you ride or die with Me, you will receive My blessing."*

God came through on His promise. Genesis tells us that:

- Abram had become very wealthy in livestock and in silver and gold. (Genesis 13:2)

- He received a new name, Abraham, and a promise of being a mighty nation. (Genesis 17:3-8)

- He made an unbreakable covenant with God, guaranteeing he would be the father to the future Messiah. (Genesis 17)

- He got to meet a pre-incarnate Jesus face to face. (Genesis 18)

- He was blessed with the birth of his long-awaited son, Isaac. (Genesis 21)

God did everything he had promised Abraham. Abraham was living in fat city. He had wealth, fame, an unbreakable covenant with God, but most importantly, he had an heir. He was 100 years old when post-menopausal Sarah miraculously gave birth to Issac. It was the one thing Abraham longed for in life. He wanted an heir so badly, someone to carry on the family name, someone to continue his legacy, a child to raise and call *"My Son."* Isaac was one loved and doted over child!

Abraham had made the decision to ride or die with God, and God honored the choice. But the story wasn't over...God had one more challenge for Abraham, one more ride or die request. You will never believe what God asks Abraham to do!

> **Some time later God tested Abraham. He said to him, "Abraham!"**
>
> **"Here I am," he replied.**

Then God said, "Take your son, your only son, whom you love—Isaac—and go to the region of Moriah. Sacrifice him there as a burnt offering on a mountain I will show you."
-Genesis 22:1-2, NIV

WHAT? How could God even ask such a thing of Abraham? Sacrifice Issac? Kill his beloved son? Destroy the one thing he loved more than anything else? How could God expect such a thing? Better yet, WHY would God expect such a thing?

I believe God was giving Abraham the ultimate ride or die test. Up until now, every time God asked Abraham to ride or die with Him, to be loyal to Him above everything else, to trust Him and obey Him even when it made no sense, it came with a promise of a blessing or prosperity. This time was different. Instead of saying to Abraham, *"If you ride or die with me, I will bless you,"* God was instead asking a new question. God basically was saying, *"Do you ride or die because of what I promised you or because you love Me?"*

This is where the rubber meets the road. What a tough request of God! I still believe God does this to us today. I believe that God still sometimes asks us to sacrifice our dreams, everything we hold dear, to Him. He will ask us to give up the dreams and desires we have deep inside of us, to sacrifice them on the altar, and say, *"Even if I don't get what I wanted out of this relationship, I will still ride or die with You."*

What did Abraham do? How did he respond to such a challenge?

Early the next morning Abraham got up and loaded his donkey. He took with him two of his servants and his son Isaac. When he had cut enough wood for the burnt offering, he set out for the place God had told him about. On the third day Abraham looked up and saw the place in the distance. He said to his servants, "Stay here with the donkey while I and the boy go over there. We will worship and then we will come back to you." - Genesis 22:3-5, NIV

Abraham made the decision to ride or die with God! Why? Because while he loved and cherished his son, he loved God even more. He would ride or die with God no matter what. Let's continue with the passage.

Abraham took the wood for the burnt offering and placed it on his son Isaac, and he himself carried the fire and the knife. As the two of them went on together, Isaac spoke up and said to his father Abraham, "Father?"

"Yes, my son?" Abraham replied.

"The fire and wood are here," Isaac said, "but where is the lamb for the burnt offering?" - Genesis 18:6-7, NIV

I am sure this question from his beloved son must have absolutely gutted Abraham. How he kept it together hearing his only child say this to him, knowing what God had asked of him, I will never know. But he was committed to God, and he trusted God knew what was best.

Abraham answered, "God himself will provide the lamb for the burnt offering, my son." And the two of them went on together.

When they reached the place God had told him about, Abraham built an altar there and arranged the wood on it.

He bound his son Isaac and laid him on the altar, on top of the wood. Then he reached out his hand and took the knife to slay his son. - Genesis 18:8-10, NIV

What a statement of faith and trust in God! Abraham did what God asked.   He would ride or die with God, even if it meant sacrificing every dream, every promise, every divine mandate God had said to him. He raised the knife over his head, and as he started to thrust the knife downwards towards everything he had ever hoped and dreamed of, his obedience was rewarded by God.

God stopped him mid knife-lunge!

But the angel of the Lord called out to him from heaven, "Abraham! Abraham!"

"Here I am," he replied.

"Do not lay a hand on the boy," he said. "Do not do anything to him. Now I know that you fear God, because you have not withheld from me your son, your only son."

Abraham looked up and there in a thicket he saw a ram caught by its horns. He went over and took the ram and sacrificed it as a burnt offering instead of his son.   So Abraham called that place The Lord Will Provide. And to this day it is said, "On the mountain of the Lord it will be provided."

The angel of the Lord called to Abraham from heaven a second time and said, "I swear by myself, declares the Lord, that because you have done this and have not withheld your son, your only son, I will surely bless you and make your descendants as numerous as the stars in the sky and as the sand on the seashore. Your descendants will take possession of the cities of their enemies, and through your offspring all nations on earth will be blessed, because you have obeyed me." - Genesis 18:11-18, NIV

God knew Abraham wasn't in it for what he could get out of it. He knew now that Abraham would ride or die with Him, no matter what it cost or what God asked.

I wonder how many of us would have been surrendered to God enough to do what Abraham did. The Bible makes it clear that Abraham, deep inside, believed that God would provide another sacrifice besides Issac, but EVEN IF HE DIDN'T, Abraham was going to obey God because he loved God above all else.

I believe God still requires His men to ride or die with Him, not just to get what they can out of the deal, but simply because they love Him, trust Him, and are loyal to Him above all else.

God still requires His men to ride or die with Him, not just to get what they can out of the deal, but simply because they love Him, trust Him, and are loyal to Him above all else.

I remember when I was a younger man in my early twenties. I thought I had my life planned all out. I would get married in Bible college, graduate, become a men's pastor at a megachurch, be a wealthy, sought after celebrity men's speaker, and then be the next Billy Graham of men's ministry, speaking to thousands (such arrogance). I knew I had a call on my life to be a men's minister, and I assumed God's call lined up with my dreams. Of course, I would ride or die with God to get this blessed life!

Then it was suddenly time to graduate. I walked down the aisle to receive my diploma without a big ministry position lined up for after graduation. As a matter of fact, I had NO position lined up. I was forced to move back home, completely humiliated. But inside, I still believed I had this grand dream coming my way. I knew how much I deserved it, and I just had to wait until everyone else realized it!

Weeks turned into months, turned into years, and still no grand dream realization. I went to God over and over and asked when He was going to do what I wanted Him to do. I wasn't ready for His answer.

God basically told me I wasn't fit to have what I wanted. I was too broken inside. I was angry. I was abusive. I had so many emotional issues inside of me that I refused to deal with that I would never be able to help others in ministry because I hadn't started working on myself. Would I allow God to work on my heart so He could use me in ministry to help others?

Basically, God asked me if I would ride or die with Him. I instantly said *"yes."* I was willing to let God do whatever He had to do to get to do the ministry I thought I was destined to do.

I let God do extreme work on my heart. I went through years of counseling. I did whatever I had to do to get God's ministry blessing. But the problem was, while I was changing and growing and becoming the man God wanted me to be, I was doing it for the wrong motivation. I was doing it so God could bless me, not simply because I loved Him and He asked me to do it.

As a result, the doors for ministry still never opened. Frustrated, I had another talk with God. I told Him that I had done everything He asked, why wasn't the big ministry opportunity opened yet? I was in no way prepared for His answer.

God spoke to me and said, *"Jamie, I want you to write down everything you want Me to do for you. Write down your ministry dreams, your personal dreams, everything you want out of life."*

I grabbed a pen and notepad, and I wrote down everything, every dream, wish, hope, and fantasy. When I was finished, I proudly went back into my prayer room and presented it to God, expecting Him to turn into the magic genie from Aladdin and give me everything I wanted. I was not ready for what He asked next.

I presented the list to God, and He said to me, *"I want you to take that list and burn it. Make it a sacrifice to Me. You need to start following and obeying Me because you love Me and because you want to, not simply to get Me to do what you want."*

Basically, God was giving me the same challenge He gave to Abraham and so many others down through the centuries. *"Do you ride or die because of what I promised you or because you love Me?"*

I was instantly convicted. I knew God was right. So I offered up my dreams in a sacrifice to Him. I lit the pages on fire and watched my dreams burn away. But I did it believing I was doing what God asked, and even though my dream wasn't **HIS** dream for my life, He knew what He was doing and would do what was best for me.

So I sacrificed my dreams to him. I didn't do it lightly. I didn't do it in a manipulative way of expecting Him to give me what I wanted because I obeyed Him. I did it honestly, presenting it as a sacrifice to Him. I let the dream die and turned my focus on becoming everything God created me to be, to becoming the man of God He destined me to be.

You know what? Unlike Abraham, God never gave me back the dream. In my case, He let the dream stay dead. Instead, He gave me a new dream, His dream. His dream wasn't formed around a desire for fame, fortune, and prestige. His dream was formed around a heart of sacrifice and service, giving everything I have to Him and others. Unlike Abraham, I didn't get back what I was willing to sacrifice. But like Abraham, I was given so much more.

It didn't happen immediately. It was a few years after that *"sacrifice"* to God until He opened doors for me. I now live my new dream every day, quietly serving others in ministry. I speak to hundreds at conferences, not thousands. Instead of a rich, cushy life, I struggle daily financially as a missionary, relying on others to support me. I am not a famous, great man, but I am God's man, doing what God called me to do. And that is enough for me.

What about you? Is God enough for you? Is serving Him and following Him simply because He asked you enough reason for you to ride or die for Him?

This doesn't always just apply to life in ministry or a job. Every person has a different one thing, something they want more than anything else in life. What is it for you?

In order for you to be a true ride or die man of God, you need to answer the question God presented to Abraham. *"Do you ride or die because of what I promised you or because you love Me?"*

Are you willing to ride or die with God even if it means that He doesn't take you on the road you expected to go? What if He asks you to sacrifice your dreams to Him? What if He asks you to give up the things in your life that you think are important but He sees as distractions or hindrances? Will you choose to lay it all on the altar, knowing there is a chance your story ends my way and not Abrahams?

It's gut-check time. Do you ride or die because of what God promised you or because you love Him? It's important to remember that Abraham gave up everything just because he loved God, not knowing he would get Isaac back. Now obviously, God never intended for Abraham to sacrifice Isaac. It's against His nature. But Abraham didn't know that. After years of waiting for a son and then years spent raising Isaac, for Abraham, this was the ultimate *"Will you ride or die with Me?"* question.

Abraham passed the test with flying colors. When it comes to giving up everything to follow God, Abraham was a rock star. He stands as an example for all of us for what it means to be a ride or die man is God. We follow his example when we say whenever, wherever, whatever God asks, the answer will always be *"Yes, because I love Him."*

Group Study Questions:

1. This chapter asked the question: *"Do we ride or die for God because of what we can get out of it, or do we do it simply because He asks us to?"* What is your honest answer?

2. Is serving God and following Him simply because He asked you enough reason for you to ride or die for Him?

3. Are you willing to ride or die with God even if it means that He doesn't take you on the road you expected to go on?

4. What if He asks you to sacrifice your dreams to Him? Will you do it?

5. What if He asks you to give up the things in your life that you think are important but He sees as distractions or hindrances? Will you obey?

6. After reading this chapter, what is one thing you will put into practice or one thing you will change in your life?

7. How can we, as a group, help you do this?

CHAPTER SEVEN

RIDE OR DIE WITH RESOLVE

But Daniel resolved not to defile himself...

I try really hard not to rant in my books, but sometimes I can't help myself. This is one of those times. I am so sick of social media! People have become so nasty to each other on social media, it is disgusting. Even some believers regularly post sentiments and political ideology that I truly think makes God cringe. They sure do make me cringe. People say and do things on social media that they would never say or do when face to face with the people their posts target. Sometimes I think believers should all change their social media passwords to *"iamachristian"* as a reminder to themselves to act like one after they sign in to their account. Ok, end of rant!

Social media has gotten out of control. Our society is being overrun with an epidemic called *"cancel culture."* A loud minority of people are trying to silence and stop a huge majority through internet bullying. One group they really, really hate are on-fire believers who know what they believe and stand firm for their beliefs. Make no mistake about it, cancel culture hates Christianity, and they are on a mission to destroy true Christians.

This is nothing new, though. There have always been people who are opposed to the ways of God, people who will try to destroy those who ride or die with resolve for God. Jesus even told His disciples that there was no way around it; the world would persecute them for following Him and doing things His way. But He also told them to rejoice in their persecution because even though the world would come after them, He had overcome the world!

God is looking for men who will ride or die with resolve. I really like that word, resolve. It means, *"a resolution or determination made, as to follow some course of action. Firmness of purpose or intent; determination."* [1]

In this chapter, we are going to look at the life of a man who was the epitome of this definition. His entire life was a life of resolve. Who is this man? Daniel.

Daniel lived during the period of time when God's judgment fell on His people. The kingdom of Judah had constantly disobeyed God and pursued the idols all around them. As a result, God sent the Babylonians to conquer them. King Nebuchadnezzar besieged Jerusalem, taking the articles of the temple of God with him. Daniel 1 also tells us that Nebuchadnezzar carried off the best and brightest princes of Judah into exile back in Babylon. Among these handsome, healthy, intelligent princes was Daniel.

Daniel was carried back to Babylon, where instantly, his resolve to ride or die with God was challenged. The Babylonians, not knowing or caring what the Jewish dietary laws were, gave food to Daniel and the other princes to eat. Daniel, who was a loyal follower of God, knew it was wrong to eat such foods, so he asked if he could follow his religious requirements. He, along with his three friends Shadrach, Meshach, and Abednego (more about them later), resolved not to defile themselves before God. As a result, they ate only allowed foods and ended up being healthier and smarter than all the other people. Daniel 1 says God blessed them with knowledge and understanding, which allowed Daniel to set himself apart in Babylon.

God continued to set Daniel apart. He helped Daniel interpret a crazy dream king Nebuchadnezzar had. This resulted in the king making Daniel the ruler over the entire province of Babylon. Daniel became part of the royal court. God used Daniel to run the kingdom of Babylon after Nebuchadnezzar's pride caused him to live seven years in a field acting like a cow (yeah, dude lost his marbles!). Daniel constantly chose to serve God and resolved to ride and die with God no matter what.

Even after God sent the Medes and Persians to defeat the Babylonians and take over the kingdom, Daniel followed and obeyed God. This resolve was amazing because there was no guarantee that a new king would cut Daniel slack for his religious resolve as the Babylonians had. But that is exactly what happened. Daniel was embraced by the new king. So that means Daniel never faced hard times because he resolved to ride or die with God, right? WRONG!

It pleased Darius to appoint 120 satraps to rule throughout the kingdom, with three administrators over them, one of whom was Daniel. The satraps were made accountable to them so that the king might not suffer loss. Now Daniel so distinguished himself among the administrators and the satraps by his exceptional qualities that the king planned to set him over the whole kingdom. At this, the administrators and the satraps tried to find grounds for charges against

Daniel in his conduct of government affairs, but they were unable to do so. - Daniel 6:1-4, NIV

Darius, the new king LOVED Daniel. The other Medes and Persian diplomats, not so much! They hated that this Jewish exile was so successful. Now the king was going to make him their boss! No way! They decided it was time to cancel Daniel. He wasn't taking their power away.

...the administrators and the satraps tried to find grounds for charges against Daniel in his conduct of government affairs, but they were unable to do so. They could find no corruption in him, because he was trustworthy and neither corrupt nor negligent. Finally these men said, "We will never find any basis for charges against this man Daniel unless it has something to do with the law of his God." -Daniel 6:4-5, NIV

Everywhere Daniel went, his commitment to follow and obey God went with him.

Wow! What a testimony! They could find no wrong or corruption in Daniel. Man, I hope this could be said of me. Daniel's resolve to ride or die with God reached every area of his life. He resolved to be a man of God at work, at home, at the backyard barbecue, at the camel races...everywhere Daniel went, his commitment to follow and obey God went with him.

These leaders knew Daniel's life was incorruptible. The only way to stop him was to go after his faith. This is exactly what they did.

So these administrators and satraps went as a group to the king and said: "May King Darius live forever! The royal administrators, prefects, satraps, advisers and governors have all agreed that the king should issue an edict and enforce the decree that anyone who prays to any god or human being during the next thirty days, except to you, Your Majesty, shall be thrown into the lions' den. Now, Your Majesty, issue the decree and put it in writing so that it cannot be altered—in accordance with the law of the Medes and Persians, which cannot be repealed." So King Darius put the decree in writing. - Daniel 6:6-9, NIV

They got the king to make a decree saying it was illegal to pray to anyone but the king. Basically, they knew Daniel was so committed to God that the only way they could touch him was to make his commitment illegal. They used Daniel's walk with God to cancel him. They told him how he had to worship.

Sound familiar? I don't know about you, but I sure do see a lot of people trying to condemn believers for their beliefs and convictions. They are saying our beliefs are too old fashioned. They are oppressive. They even say we are hateful and promote hate speech. They say we are wrong to say that:

- Following Jesus is the only way to get to Heaven.

- People who don't accept Christ will go to Hell.

- Good people can go to Hell.

- Islam, Hinduism, and all other religions are false religions, and even the most devoted followers won't get into Heaven unless they leave this religion and accept Christ.

- All sex outside of marriage is sin, including marital affairs, homosexuality, and pre-marital sex.

- Abortion is murder.

- There are moral absolutes.

The list could go on and on. The world adamantly hates these beliefs, and they say Christians are old-fashioned at best, hateful bigots at worst.

Even more dangerous is the new religious movement of Progressive Christianity. This movement so longs for the approval and acceptance of the world that they are twisting and distorting the teachings and principles of the Bible. They are casting off the basic doctrinal beliefs that Christianity is founded on and rewriting Scripture to make it say what they want it to say. They reject the Old Testament because a loving God could never have done the things the Old Testament says God did. They reject the teaching of Paul because he doesn't line up with their moral agenda. They basically only like the teachings of Jesus, and even then, they really pick and choose which ones they like.

The Progressive Christian agenda is finding fertile soil among the younger people today. So much of their beliefs coincide with the teaching that young people receive in public schools and universities. Our teens and twenties are buying into it. Parents, not wanting to risk losing their kids or grandkids, are going along with this agenda. Slowly, this false doctrine is gaining popularity. But it is so dangerous because it is not Biblical.

Progressive Christianity:

- Rejects the idea of God requiring Jesus to die for our sins…they call that cosmic child abuse.

- They believe that no loving God would do such a thing and that it isn't even necessary because we are all innately good, and God is loving and never would condemn us for sin.

- They reject the idea of hell. God would never send anyone to hell. He is a loving God. They believe Heaven is not where we are made perfect, but it is the realization of the perfection we already have.

- Progressive Christianity teaches that there don't have to be moral norms. They completely embrace the LGBTQ platform. They promote sex in any form at any time with anyone because God created sex to be enjoyed. Any teaching in churches to the contrary is just old fashioned systematic suppression of women.

- Because sex often has consequences, they are pro-abortion. They believe a woman has the right to enjoy sex however she chooses and should not have to suffer any consequences of this action. So she should abort any unwanted babies.

- The Progressive Christians embrace social justice causes like BLM, socialism, and environmentalism. They say Jesus wasn't the son of God, He was simply a good man who stood up against the social injustices of His time, and we are called to do the same.

John Cooper, the lead singer of Skillet and host of the *"Cooper Stuff"* Podcast, calls this chasing the approval of the world *"chasing woke cookies."** These Progressive Christians want the title of Christian, but they also want the approval of the woke crowd.

I believe Progressive Christianity is the biggest threat facing the church today.

I really believe that in the future true believers will face persecution from Progressive Christians. They and the world will say, *"You don't do what you do or believe what you believe because you are a Christian. It's because you are racist, or hateful, or homophobic, or oppressive. We are Christians, and we don't promote the hateful things you believe."*

You can see this coming a mile away. It will happen, and we will have to decide if we are going to let society tell us how to worship and what to believe. This is why it is so important for men of God to commit to riding or dying with resolve.

1. Choose who you will serve.

Daniel had to choose if he would obey what society told him to do or what God told him to do. What did he do?

> *Now when Daniel learned that the decree had been published, he went home to his upstairs room where the windows opened toward Jerusalem. Three times a day he got down on his knees and prayed, giving thanks to his God, just as he had done before.* - *Daniel 6:10, NIV*

When the world says, "You can't say that" or "You can't do that," will you submit to mob culture or do it God's way?

No one was going to stop Daniel from obeying and serving God! He had resolved many years ago that He would ride or die with God, and this time was no different. I don't think Daniel even hesitated. He was so sold out to God and had made this stand so many times before that it was part of his nature. No matter the consequences, he would ride or die with God.

Who are you going to ride or die with? When the world says, "*You can't say that*" or "*You can't do that,*" will you submit to mob culture or do it God's way? Like Joshua challenged the people of Israel so many years before, you have to choose who you will serve, the gods of culture or the true God Who saved you and set you free.

It's a choice everyone has to eventually make. What will you choose? (Joshua 24:15)

Faced with this choice, Daniel chose to ride or die with God.

2. Understand the cost of your choice.

Daniel made his decision. As a result, his enemies backed off, he got the promotion as leader of the kingdom, and everything worked out fine, right? Wrong!

The men who set a trap for Daniel watched him closely to catch him praying. They knew he would never go against God, so they waited to grab him. They found him praying and immediately went to tell the king. They reminded him of his edict and the punishment that breaking it would bring. With all of this fresh in the king's mind, they threw Daniel under the bus.

> *Then they said to the king, "Daniel, who is one of the exiles from Judah, pays no attention to you, Your Majesty, or to the decree you put in writing. He still prays three times a day." - Daniel 6:13, NIV*

Immediately, Darius's heart sank. He loved Daniel. Remember, he planned on making Daniel the boss, directly under him. He wanted to save Daniel, but it was out of his hands.

> *When the king heard this, he was greatly distressed; he was determined to rescue Daniel and made every effort until sundown to save him.*
>
> *Then the men went as a group to King Darius and said to him, "Remember, Your Majesty, that according to the law of the Medes and Persians no decree or edict that the king issues can be changed." - Daniel 6:14-15, NIV*

It was an irreversible law. The king had no choice but to send Daniel to his death.

> *So the king gave the order, and they brought Daniel and threw him into the lions' den. The king said to Daniel, "May your God, whom you serve continually, rescue you!" - Daniel 6:16, NIV*

Wait, what?? Daniel did the right thing! He decided to ride or die with God. How could this happen?

Well, unfortunately, when you choose to ride or die with someone, death is sometimes the outcome. But when you are so loyal, so faithful, and so committed to God, death is not feared or dreaded.

You need to know that sometimes you will suffer persecution and hard times when you resolve to follow God. History is filled with stories of God miraculously moving mountains to save those who choose to ride or die with Him. But it is also filled with stories of people who suffered for their resolve, facing the ultimate punishment of death. Your resolve could have a price.

I recently read about a woman who ran a flower shop. She had loyal customers who she considered friends. Then one day, they asked her to do the flowers for their same sex-wedding, and she refused. They sued her and took her to court in a case very similar to the famous case of the baker who refused to bake a wedding cake for such a wedding. In that case, he won the legal fight and was rewarded by his ride or die resolve to do things God's way. But in this florist case, she lost the legal battle. Two similar situations where people resolved to ride or die for God and His ways. One was vindicated, but one lost. Does she regret her decision? No. In a Fox News article, she is quoted as saying:

"Sure, I want to win, and yes, I want everything to go smooth, but He doesn't promise that," she said. "He just says be obedient and be faithful, and that's what we're supposed to do. I mean, it's just a trust level all the way around. If you don't trust in God's word, then you don't have anything to trust in....We all have to figure out where our line is that we won't cross... I will say that if they do follow Christ, that He will supply all their needs and He will give them the strength and the courage and whatever it takes." [1]

No regrets there! She knew it could cost her something to ride or die with resolve, and she was willing to pay the price. She knew what we will see in our final point.

3. God will honor our decision and use it to further His kingdom.

Daniel knew there would be a price to pay for the decision he made. He also knew God would honor his decision and use it to advance His kingdom, whether he lived or died.

Daniel 6 says King Darius tossed and turned all night, wondering if Daniel's God would come through. At the crack of daylight, the king went to the lion's den and had the cover removed.

When he came near the den, he called to Daniel in an anguished voice, "Daniel, servant of the living God, has your God, whom you serve continually, been able to rescue you from the lions?"

Daniel answered, "May the king live forever! My God sent his angel, and he shut the mouths of the lions. They have not hurt me, because I was found innocent in his sight. Nor have I ever done any wrong before you, Your Majesty." - Daniel 6:20-22, NIV

Daniel's resolve to ride or die with God caused the king and everyone else to know that God really was the one and only God. He shut the lion's mouths and saved Daniel. Everyone in Babylon heard about it and saw that God was the one true God. Daniel was lifted out of the lion's den without a single scratch. Then it says that the king ordered the men who trapped Daniel to take his place in the lion's den.

> *At the king's command, the men who had falsely accused Daniel were brought in and thrown into the lions' den... And before they reached the floor of the den, the lions overpowered them and crushed all their bones. -Daniel 6:24, NIV*

This removed any and all doubt that it was God who had saved Daniel. The lions weren't on a diet. They didn't touch Daniel, but they ravished these troublemakers mid-drop. It wasn't that the lions weren't hungry. God had saved Daniel. And now everyone knew it.

> *Then King Darius wrote to all the nations and peoples of every language in all the earth:*
>
> *"May you prosper greatly! I issue a decree that in every part of my kingdom people must fear and reverence the God of Daniel.*
>
> *For he is the living God and he endures forever; his kingdom will not be destroyed, his dominion will never end.*
>
> *He rescues and he saves he performs signs and wonders in the heavens and on the earth. He has rescued Daniel from the power of the lions."*
>
> *So Daniel prospered during the reign of Darius and the reign of Cyrus the Persian. - Daniel 6:25-28, NIV*

Daniel's resolve to ride or die caused the world to hear about the greatness and power of God. Because Daniel resolved to ride or die with God no matter what, God's kingdom was lauded by the biggest earthly kingdom of the day.

Guys, I can't emphasize it enough. You have no idea what your decision to ride or die with resolve will accomplish for God's kingdom. I guarantee you, you will not win any *"woke cookies"* from the world or from Progressive Christianity for standing firm for what you know to be true, but God will always

I guarantee you, you will not win any woke cookies from the world or from Progressive Christianity for standing firm for what you know to be true, but God will always honor your choice.

honor your choice. Whether in victory in life or victory through death, God's kingdom will endure when you resolve to ride or die for God.

The question boils down to this. Do you want the approval of men or the approval of God? In my opinion, there isn't really a choice. Losing the approval of men may cause temporary problems or persecution, but losing the approval of God can have eternal consequences. Which one will you choose? I hope you choose to ride or die with resolve for God and His ways.

Group Study Questions:

1. This chapter stated: *"Everywhere Daniel went, his commitment to follow and obey God went with him."* Can you say the same about yourself?

2. Daniel had people try and tell him how to serve God. How do you see this happening today?

3. What is the danger of Progressive Christianity? How can you avoid its trap and help others do the same?

4. When the world says, *"You can't say that"* or *"You can't do that,"* will you submit to mob culture, or do it God's ways, no matter the results?

5. Will you resolve today to serve and obey God even if it goes against the culture and even if it causes persecution?

6. After reading this chapter, what is one thing you will put into practice or one thing you will change in your life?

7. How can we, as a group, help you do this?

CHAPTER EIGHT

RIDE OR DIE WITH FAITH

If we are thrown into the blazing furnace, the God we serve is able to deliver us from it, and he will deliver us from Your Majesty's hand.

Did you go to Sunday school as a kid? My parents took me to Sunday school every week. I can still remember going to the classroom and being mesmerized by the Bible stories that were told, illustrated by the old-school felt board. If you are too young to know what a felt board is, it was a small board that was made of felt, and there were cutouts of the characters that were placed on the felt to illustrate the stories. It's how teachers taught Bible stories before computers and the internet..yes, I am old!

Anyway, I loved hearing the great stories of men and women in the Bible who were committed to loving and serving God and the miraculous ways God helped them. It is probably where I first fell in love with the concept of riding or dying. I just didn't realize then what it was. As a child, they were just miraculous stories of God showing His power.

Many churches no longer have Sunday school, and this breaks my heart. Children need to know the stories of God's might and power. They need to be as mesmerized by Bible stories as I was as a kid. Get your kids into Sunday school! But back to this chapter.

One of my favorite stories from those felt boards is the story we are going to look at in this chapter. It is the story of three men who had to choose if they would ride or die with God to the point of death or betray God to save their own skin.

In the chapter about Daniel, we mentioned his three friends, Shadrach, Meshach, and Abednego. Like Daniel, these three young men when were carried off in exile to Babylon. They stood shoulder to shoulder and risked their lives with Daniel when they all decided they couldn't eat the forbidden food. God rewarded their stand by making them smarter and healthier than all who ate what they were given.

After Daniel was promoted for telling King Nebuchadnezzar the meaning of his dream, Daniel promoted his three pals and made them administrators over the province of Babylon. They served the kingdom faithfully, working for its best interest, but even after the promotion, they still lived a life of ride or die with God. They worked for Babylon, but they worshipped and served God. Nothing or no one would cause these three men to turn their backs on God. This resolve was soon tested.

> *King Nebuchadnezzar made an image of gold, sixty cubits high and six cubits wide, and set it up on the plain of Dura in the province of Babylon. He then summoned the satraps, prefects, governors, advisers, treasurers, judges, magistrates and all the other provincial officials to come to the*

dedication of the image he had set up.   So the satraps, prefects, governors, advisers, treasurers, judges, magistrates and all the other provincial officials assembled for the dedication of the image that King Nebuchadnezzar had set up, and they stood before it.

Then the herald loudly proclaimed, "Nations and peoples of every language, this is what you are commanded to do: As soon as you hear the sound of the horn, flute, zither, lyre, harp, pipe and all kinds of music, you must fall down and worship the image of gold that King Nebuchadnezzar has set up. Whoever does not fall down and worship will immediately be thrown into a blazing furnace." - Daniel 3:1-6, NIV

Old Neb made a law that if you didn't bow to his idol and worship it, you would be thrown into a fiery furnace.   Shadrach, Meshach, and Abednego now had a choice to make. Were they going to ride or die with God or compromise and save their skin? You can probably figure out what they chose.

Therefore, as soon as they heard the sound of the horn, flute, zither, lyre, harp and all kinds of music, all the nations and peoples of every language fell down and worshiped the image of gold that King Nebuchadnezzar had set up.

At this time some astrologers came forward and denounced the Jews. They said to King Nebuchadnezzar, "May the king live forever! Your Majesty has issued a decree that everyone who hears the sound of the horn, flute, zither, lyre, harp, pipe and all kinds of music must fall down and worship the image of gold, and that whoever does not fall down and worship will be thrown into a blazing furnace. But there are some Jews whom you have set over the affairs of the

province of Babylon—Shadrach, Meshach and Abednego— who pay no attention to you, Your Majesty. They neither serve your gods nor worship the image of gold you have set up." -Daniel 3:7-12, NIV

They refused to bow! They knew the only reason they were in Babylon in the first place was that their ancestors had bowed and worshipped idols. The nation was judged because of its idolatry. They could have lived in fat city back in Jerusalem if their ancestors had just rejected idols, refused to bow, and served God properly. They were blessed to have survived the siege and even more blessed to be chosen to go to Babylon as exiles. They were not about to worship an idol. They would ride or die with God!

This brings us to our first point.

1. We must reject all idols.

Like our three heroes in this chapter, we must choose to reject all idol worship.

"Of course, we don't worship idols or foreign gods in America. You mean we need to be careful that we don't make other things idols in our hearts."

No, I mean we must reject all idols. Yes, we can make idols out of things in our life like sports, movie stars, money, or friends. There are also different ways to set things before God and make them idols in our hearts. Most of us scoff at the idea of worshipping real idols. Obviously, we don't worship idols or foreign gods.

I disagree with this. It's no longer "*obvious*" that we don't worship idols or participate in foreign religions.

Instead, it is all too common for Christians to mix serving God and going to church on Sunday with participating in foreign religion and idol worship during the week.

Don't believe me? Think I'm crazy?   Consider this:

We now live in a society that says all religions are equal.   We talked about this in our chapter on Daniel. As Buddhism, Hinduism, Animism, and other foreign religions have become the cultural norm, their practices have become "*hobbies*" within Christianity.

- It's now commonplace to hear about Christians doing yoga, even though it is derived from Hinduism.

- Many follow the practice of meditation as laid out by Buddhism.

- Many believe in crystals' healing power and set them around their house, even though this is New Age theology.

- Marie Kondo had people thanking objects before they threw them out which is Animism.

- Christians dabble in the occult by playing Dungeons and Dragons and Ouiji boards.

- Nobody even blinks an eye when Christians know their astrological sign or read their horoscope.

- Christians watch television shows about demons and the occult on television all the time. Churches promote Harry Potter and Lord of the Rings without realizing the real life dangers of magic and the occult.

- We talk about Kharma, read the writings of Gandhi and other Eastern philosophers as if they aren't false teachers preaching false religions.

The fact is that the Christian church has a problem they don't want to talk about when it comes to worshiping foreign gods and idol worship. However, just like in the days of the prophets, today, the same loving God says, "*I don't want you to suffer the consequences of these sins. It's time to recognize your sin, repent, stop worshipping idols, and participating in foreign religions."*

These things may seem harmless, but they are idol worship. We need to reject them completely. Don't entertain them at all.

God is calling us back to the truth that we are to serve God and serve Him only.

I believe we need to search our hearts and see if there is even a hint of participating in foreign religions or idol worship in our lives.

Like the Israelites, today, the choice stands before each of us: will we follow God and abandon idols and foreign religions?

We need to search our hearts and see if there is even a hint of participating in foreign religions or idol worship in our lives.

If we say *"yes,"* then we have to follow it up with actions.

I know I have had to make changes in my life. I have always loved the Marvel movies, you know, Iron Man, Captain America, and the rest of earth's mightiest heroes. But recently, Marvel has been introducing a lot of Buddhism and magic into their movies. Just today, the teaser trailer for the third Spiderman movie was released, and it all centers on spells, magic, witchcraft, and the Buddhist worship of Dr. Strange. I do not want to give any credence to witchcraft, Buddhism, or any eastern religion in my life, so I will not be watching this movie. I made the same decision when they released Dr. Strange because he is a warlock. I didn't watch Wandavision because Wanda is a witch. I don't want to allow idolatry into my life in any way. So I don't participate.

I encourage you to do the same. Stop doing yoga and meditation. Throw out the demonic games. Stop watching and reading all movies, tv shows, and books that promote these false religions and satanic work.

Yes, you may suffer for rejecting this. People may call you old-fashioned. They may say your stance is ridiculous. They may even throw the old *"Freedom in Christ"* verse at you to justify their compromise. But I encourage you, stand strong, resist idols, and commit to serving God and God alone.

2. We must choose that, no matter the consequences, we will not compromise.

Sometimes choosing to stand firm against culture and the ways of man will cause you to face the consequences. No matter the consequences, we cannot compromise. This is exactly what Shadrach, Meshach, and Abednego chose to do. They would not bow to anyone but God.

> *Furious with rage, Nebuchadnezzar summoned Shadrach, Meshach and Abednego. So these men were brought before the king, and Nebuchadnezzar said to them, "Is it true, Shadrach, Meshach and Abednego, that you do not serve my gods or worship the image of gold I have set up? Now when you hear the sound of the horn, flute, zither, lyre, harp, pipe and all kinds of music, if you are ready to fall down and worship the image I made, very good. But if you do not worship it, you will be thrown immediately into a blazing furnace. Then what god will be able to rescue you from my hand?" - Daniel 6:13-15, NIV*

Old Neb was furious. How dare they defy him like this? But Shadrach, Meshach, and Abednego had been faithful servants over the years, so he decided to give them one more chance. But they didn't need another chance…they refused to bow.

> *Shadrach, Meshach and Abednego replied to him, "King Nebuchadnezzar, we do not need to defend ourselves before you in this matter. If we are thrown into the blazing furnace, the God we serve is able to deliver us from it, and he will deliver us from Your Majesty's hand. But even if he does not, we want you to know, Your Majesty, that we will not serve your gods or worship the image of gold you have set up." - Daniel 6:16-18, NIV*

What faith! What belief in God! They believed that God would reward them and rescue them from the fire. But I love the second part of this verse even more…let's read it again.

> *But even if he does not, we want you to know, Your Majesty, that we will not serve your gods or worship the image of gold you have set up. -Daniel 3:18, NIV*

Even if He doesn't, we will not bow! Wow! I applaud this faith and devotion. They believed God would come through for them, but even if He didn't…even if God left them hanging, even if God turned away from them, even if they burned to a crisp, they would not abandon God and bow to the idol. They would ride or die with God, no matter what!

I don't know if we truly understand how great this statement is. I personally didn't until recently. In the opening of this book, I talked about how hard the past few months have been. It has truly been one of the most difficult times I have ever faced. The temptation to quit and walk away was never so strong. I have never been so discouraged. I had a huge obstacle standing in my life, something I never saw coming, something that shook me to my very core. It made me question whether God really had my back.

Would God help me face this hard time? Could I trust Him? He allowed it to happen. Would He help me go through it? Would He give me the strength to cope? I begged God daily to end the situation, to take this obstacle away permanently, to give us freedom from it, and to let us live happily once again. Daily I begged God, and daily the situation intensified instead of easing.

Then I remembered this story of Shadrach, Meshach, and Abednego. I reread these words, ***"Even if He doesn't, we will not bow."***

I realized at this moment, I had to make the same choice. In tears, I said to God, *"I hate that You have allowed this into my life. I can't stand living like this any longer. I want You to do something different. But even if You don't, I will follow You."*

Surrendering my will like this was one of the hardest things I ever had to do. I didn't want to do it, but I knew I had to do it. The situation didn't go away, but my horrible attitude did because I chose that, no matter what pain I faced or what I had to endure, I will not walk away from God. No matter the consequences, I would not compromise. I would ride or die with God, no matter what.

I don't know what you are facing today, but I encourage you to adopt Shadrach, Meshach, and Abednego's ride or die attitude that nothing and no one will cause you to walk away from God. Even if God doesn't come through, make the choice not to bow.

Our three friends made this choice. What was the outcome?

Then Nebuchadnezzar was furious with Shadrach, Meshach and Abednego, and his attitude toward them changed. He ordered the furnace heated seven times hotter than usual and commanded some of the strongest soldiers in his army to tie up Shadrach, Meshach and Abednego and throw them into the blazing furnace. So these men, wearing their robes, trousers, turbans and other clothes, were bound and thrown into the blazing furnace. The king's command was so urgent and the furnace so hot that the flames of the fire killed the soldiers who took up Shadrach, Meshach and Abednego, and these three men, firmly tied, fell into the blazing furnace. - Daniel 6:19-23, NIV

The old felt board story showed Shadrach, Meshach, and Abednego standing with little campfires around their feet. This was a gross understatement of what they faced. The fire was so big and hot that it instantly killed the three soldiers who got close to it to throw our three guys in.   Our three ride or die men should have died instantly as well. But we read something different.

Then King Nebuchadnezzar leaped to his feet in amazement and asked his advisers, "Weren't there three men that we tied up and threw into the fire?"

They replied, "Certainly, Your Majesty."

He said, "Look! I see four men walking around in the fire, unbound and unharmed, and the fourth looks like a son of the gods." - **Daniel 6:24-25, NIV**

Shadrach, Meshach, and Abednego survived the fire. They didn't burn to death from the flame. They didn't suffocate from smoke inhalation. Instead, they walked freely around the fire. The ropes that bound them were gone, and they were safe. Even more, they were not alone. Jesus, Himself, was in the fire with them. This brings us to our third point.

3. *When we ride or die for God, He will ride or die for us.*

God will always be with you through the furnace. When you choose to ride or die with God, He will ride or die with you. Even though your choices have consequences, He will be with you and give you the strength to endure the consequences of standing for Him.

Shadrach, Meshach, and Abednego choose to believe God was going to honor their ride or die attitude, but even if He didn't rescue them, they would do it anyway. Not only did God rescue them, but He also went through the trial with them. He did it to honor their stand but also to build His kingdom.

When you choose to ride or die with God, He will ride or die with you.

> *Nebuchadnezzar then approached the opening of the blazing furnace and shouted, "Shadrach, Meshach and Abednego, servants of the Most High God, come out! Come here!"*
>
> *So Shadrach, Meshach and Abednego came out of the fire, and the satraps, prefects, governors and royal advisers crowded around them. They saw that the fire had not harmed their bodies, nor was a hair of their heads singed; their robes were not scorched, and there was no smell of fire on them.*

Then Nebuchadnezzar said, "Praise be to the God of Shadrach, Meshach and Abednego, who has sent his angel and rescued his servants! They trusted in him and defied the king's command and were willing to give up their lives rather than serve or worship any god except their own God. Therefore I decree that the people of any nation or language who say anything against the God of Shadrach, Meshach and Abednego be cut into pieces and their houses be turned into piles of rubble, for no other god can save in this way."

Then the king promoted Shadrach, Meshach and Abednego in the province of Babylon. - Daniel 6:26-30

Guys, It won't always be easy to ride or die with faith. The times you have the least reason to believe are the times you need to ride or die with faith in God the most. Our three pals saw the flames. They felt the heat. They had no reason to believe that God would save them. But they believed anyway.

They even believed that standing in faith was worth it, even if God left them hanging. Why? Because they not only had faith that God would take care of them on earth, but they also had faith to believe God would take care of them in eternity. So whether they lived or were fried in the furnace, God would have their backs either way. They were saved, and God was glorified throughout Babylon.

Guys, they knew what we need to understand. Riding or dying in faith could cost you everything here on earth, but God will never leave you or forsake you. He will always do what is best for His children and His Kingdom. God was in the flame with them. He had their backs. He is right there in the middle of whatever hard situation you are facing. He has your back. When we choose to ride or die with God, He will always ride and die with us.

Where are you today? Are you confidently following God, sure that He will ride or die with you?

Are you a man of faith? Maybe your faith is wavering. Maybe you could relate to what I shared about my life as you face what seems like an impossible situation. Are you struggling to just make it through the day as you battle your own fiery furnace? I encourage you, follow Shadrach, Meshach, and Abednego's example and surrender it all to God. Admit that you truly hope God rescues you from this situation, but even if He doesn't, you will surrender to Him. This takes as much of a ride or die with faith attitude as any bold statement that God will come through. You have it in you. If I can do it, so can you.

We must all follow the example of Shadrach, Meshach, and Abednego. No matter what we face, we will not bow. We will allow no idols in our lives. No matter the consequences, we will not compromise. We will be men of faith who believe that when we ride or die with God, He will ride or die with us.

Group Study Questions:

1. Are you allowing any foreign religions or idols in your life? If so, will you commit to removing them?

2. Shadrach, Meshack, and Abednego committed to obeying God even if God didn't come through for them. Will you make the same choice not to bow even if God doesn't come through and do what you want?

3. This chapter stated: *"Riding or dying in faith could cost you everything here on earth, but God will never leave you or forsake you."* What does this mean to you?

4. What scares you most about riding or dying in faith?

5. Is it a rational fear? Is it worth not obeying God?

6. After reading this chapter, what is one thing you will put into practice or one thing you will change in your life?

7. How can we, as a group, help you do this?

CHAPTER NINE

RIDE OR DIE THROUGH DISCOURAGEMENT

I am the only one left, and now they are trying to kill me too.

When I was a kid, every Saturday night at our house consisted of my dad watching Bob Villa on *This Old House*, *The Lawrence Welk Show*, and *Hee Haw*. I hated it. I use to always whine, *"Can't we watch something else? This is so boring."* Now that I'm an adult, I keep catching myself watching HGTV and DIY Network. I guess that's what happens. Anyways, *Hee Haw* had a song on it that I've been thinking about lately.

The song would be sung by four or five hillbillies sitting around singing about their troubles. The song was *"Gloom, Despair, and Agony on Me."* Usually, the verses depicted some silly crisis each one was facing in their lives that wasn't really a crisis, but then they'd sing the chorus about feeling gloom, despair, agony, depression, and misery.

This song was always funny, but it also highlights how discouragement can defeat God's men. One of the biggest traps I see men of God fall into is feeling discouraged. They feel they are the only men trying to follow God and live according to His standards. The enemy makes them feel like they shouldn't even bother trying. He gets too many men to abandon their pursuit of riding or dying with God by making them think they are the only one even trying to because it is impossible to do. He gets their eyes off of what God is doing and onto the struggles and hard times they are facing.

In this chapter, I want to look at a man who was riding or dying for God but who began to struggle with feeling isolated and alone. Then he experiences God in a rare and unexpected way and finds what we all need when feeling discouraged...hope, and the renewed determination to ride or die with Him. Let's look at the life of Elijah.

Elijah was a prophet to the nation of Israel. We first read about Elijah during the reign of Ahab, King of Israel. Elijah was sent by God to constantly warn Ahab to stop worshipping the god of Baal. Ahab despised Elijah, especially after Elijah's prophecy that God was going to send a drought on the land to judge Ahab and Israel for their sins. Elijah spent a lot of his time on the run from Ahab and his wife, Jezebel, as they constantly sought to kill him. For three years, he went wherever God sent him as God provided for his daily needs.

After three years of living on the run through the drought, God told Elijah to go back to Israel.

After a long time, in the third year, the word of the Lord came to Elijah: "Go and present yourself to Ahab, and I

will send rain on the land." So Elijah went to present himself to Ahab. -1 Kings 18:1-2, NIV

We read in the following verses that a follower of God named Obadiah was working frantically to rescue the prophets of God from extermination at the hand of Jezebel and hide them. Elijah found Obadiah and got him to negotiate a meeting between Elijah and Ahab.

> *Obadiah went to meet Ahab and told him, and Ahab went to meet Elijah. When he saw Elijah, he said to him, "Is that you, you troubler of Israel?"*
>
> *"I have not made trouble for Israel," Elijah replied. "But you and your father's family have. You have abandoned the Lord's commands and have followed the Baals. Now summon the people from all over Israel to meet me on Mount Carmel. And bring the four hundred and fifty prophets of Baal and the four hundred prophets of Asherah, who eat at Jezebel's table." - 1 Kings 18:16-19, NIV*

Now we have some action! Like the gunfight at the O.K. Corral, Ahab and the Baal prophets were going to battle it out with Elijah. Elijah went to King Ahab and challenged him to the ultimate face-off to prove whose God was more powerful. He challenged King Ahab to build an altar to Baal, and Elijah would build an altar to God. They would both get an animal and put it on the altar for the sacrifice. Then each would pray to their God, Elijah to the real God, and the Baal prophets to Baal, and ask them to send fire to burn the sacrifice. Whichever sacrifice caught fire would be the winner and would prove whose God was true.

King Ahab had to agree. He wasn't going to let Elijah challenge him like this without responding. So first thing in the morning King Ahab and his fellow Baal worshippers climbed to the top of Mt.

Carmel with Elijah and his servant. As always happens with events like this, lots of people followed them to see the show.

When they got to the top, King Ahab's men immediately began to build their altar. They gathered big rocks and piled them one on top of another. Then they piled pieces of wood on top of the rocks and placed their animal on top of the wood. They began dancing and praying around the altar, asking Baal to light the sacrifice on fire.

They danced and prayed for hours, but no fire. Elijah, bored with the ridiculous display, began to tease the Baal worshippers. *"Maybe you need to yell louder...maybe Baal is asleep,"* he yelled. This made the Baal worshippers angry, so they prayed even louder. Then Elijah said, *"Maybe he is going to the bathroom and is too busy to help you. Better call louder."* Still nothing.

They began cutting themselves with knives to show Baal they were serious. Now they were hot, tired, dirty, bloody, and thirsty. Remember, they didn't have very much water because of the drought. They danced all day long, for eight whole hours, but Baal never sent fire to burn the altar.

Finally, Elijah stood up and told them their time was up. Now it was his turn to try. He gathered twelve large stones, one for each of the cities in Israel, and piled them on top of each other to build the altar. Then, like the Baal worshippers, he put wood on top of the altar and then placed his sacrifice on top. However, he didn't stop there.

Elijah took a shovel and dug a trench all around the sacrifice. This was unusual when it came to building an altar, and it raised a few eyebrows. However, what he did next stunned everyone.

Elijah asked the people to go and get twelve barrels of water, almost all the water that was left in the country. When the servant came back, Elijah told him to pour the barrels of water over the altar, the wood, and the sacrifice. Everyone thought Elijah had gone crazy! How was God supposed to light his sacrifice on fire if it was soaking wet! It was impossible! There was no way fire could burn the soaking wet altar and sacrifice.

However, Elijah was not worried. He knew he served the One True God Who had the power to do anything, even burn a soaking wet sacrifice. He got down to his knees, looked toward heaven, and said, *"LORD, let it be known today that you are God in Israel and that I am your servant and have done all these things at your command. Answer me, LORD, answer me, so these people will know that you, LORD, are God, and that you are turning their hearts back again." - 1 Kings 18:36-37, NIV*

At that very moment, fire shot down from the sky. It consumed the altar and the sacrifice. It even burnt up the water in the trench around the altar. It was a miracle! God proved He was the only true God. Baal wasn't God, He was!

When all the people who were watching saw the fire fly out of the sky and consume everything, they fell to their knees and yelled, *"The Lord, He is God, The Lord He is God!"* They were convinced. They knew Baal had no power, God had the power. They immediately realized they were wrong to have followed King Ahab. They repented and followed God and killed every Baal prophet who had lead them astray.

Now that the people had come back to worship Him, God no longer was angry. He sent a very tiny cloud, the size of a hand, and it rained, and all the rivers and streams were filled with water again. God's punishment of no rain ended when the Israelites returned to loving and serving Him again.

So Elijah, a man who was a wholehearted ride or die, follower of God, won the battle. People repented, and rain fell again. Everyone loved Elijah, and he was a local hero, right? Wrong!

> *Now Ahab told Jezebel everything Elijah had done and how he had killed all the prophets with the sword. So Jezebel sent a messenger to Elijah to say, "May the gods deal with me, be it ever so severely, if by this time tomorrow I do not make your life like that of one of them."*
> *- 1 Kings 19:1-2, NIV*

Jezebel was outraged. As a life-long Baal worshipper who was named after one of the chants used at Baal worship, she vowed to kill Elijah for what he had done to Baal worship in Israel.

Now, of course, Elijah was flying high from his victory. For three years, God had provided daily for Elijah, keeping him safe. Now God had used Elijah to win a mighty victory in Israel. There was no way he would be scared of Jezebel's threats! Again, wrong!

> *Elijah was afraid and ran for his life. When he came to Beersheba in Judah, he left his servant there, while he himself went a day's journey into the wilderness. He came to a broom bush, sat down under it and prayed that he might die. "I have had enough, Lord," he said. "Take my life; I am no better than my ancestors." Then he lay down under the bush and fell asleep. - 1 Kings 19:3-5, NIV*

Talk about going from the highest of highs to the lowest of lows! In a matter of hours, he went from a mighty victory on the mountain to a defeated, almost suicidal place, hiding in the desert. What happened??

Often believers face their greatest spiritual attacks after their greatest victories. Elijah had dealt a deadly blow against the demonic forces of Baal, and they were fighting back. The good news? Even when feeling defeated and discouraged, God still took care of Elijah.

> *All at once an angel touched him and said, "Get up and eat." He looked around, and there by his head was some bread baked over hot coals, and a jar of water. He ate and drank and then lay down again. - 1 Kings 19:5-6, NIV*

I love this verse. Notice God didn't get angry with Elijah. He didn't scold him or say, *"I thought you were Mr. Ride or Die?!? I gave you a great victory, and now you act like this?"* No instead, God took care of Elijah. He provided for Him. He fed him. He gave him rest and helped him get enough strength to get back up and go to Mount Horeb, God's mountain.

Often believers face their greatest spiritual attacks after their greatest victories.

An exhausted, defeated Elijah made a forty-day trek to God's mountain. It is here that we start to hear what was on Elijah's mind.

> *The word of the Lord came to him: "What are you doing here, Elijah?"*
>
> *He replied, "I have been very zealous for the Lord God Almighty. The Israelites have rejected your covenant, torn down your altars, and put your prophets to death with the sword. I am the only one left, and now they are trying to kill me too." - 1 Kings 19:9-10, NIV*

Elijah told God he felt alone. He had served God wholeheartedly. He chose to ride or die for God. But in his mind, it left him exhausted, scared, and alone.

Basically, Elijah is saying, *"I did it Your way. I live my life for You. I am the only one who is doing that. I am all alone, they are trying to destroy me, and I can't keep doing this by myself."*

The enemy loves making men of God feel alone and isolated. When he does this, he is able to start playing mind games in our heads.

I have been honest in this book about struggles I have faced this year, and I am going to do it again. Coming off of our 2021 Mantour Conferences, I struggled with feeling exactly like Elijah. We faced so much opposition to doing our conferences in 2021 coming out of the Covid shutdown. I had so many people telling me not to do Mantour conferences this year or to do them virtually. People told me no one would come. They said to expect at best 25% of the normal turnout we received. I had so much discouragement thrown my way.

However, I felt God leading me to do in-person conferences. It was a terrifying step of faith to go against the advice of so many people, but I knew God had told me to go forward. I chose to ride or die in obedience to do what He told me to do.

We ended up having a fabulous year of conferences. Losses in attendance were barely noticeable. The attitude of the men who attended was the best we ever experienced as they came excited and expecting God to move. We had men accept Christ. Men were coming to the altar and getting right with God. It was one of our best years ever!

When the conferences ended, I found myself struggling heavily with discouragement, exhaustion, and fears. Instead of coming out victorious, I came out wondering why I even bothered doing what I do. That makes zero sense, but it was where I was spiritually, mentally, and emotionally. When you combine this with all the other struggles I previously alluded to that happened prior to the conferences in 2021, I was left feeling alone and defeated. I. Was. Done.

I struggled with this for weeks. Adessa kept pleading with me to take some time off and get rested and refocused. But I refused. My mood was spreading and affecting everyone around me. It all came to a head during a contentious meeting with a trusted advisor in which he thought tough love was what I needed, but instead, it left me in tears on our zoom call.

Eventually, someone was able to get through to me. My missionary supervisor and mentor told me that I needed to walk away for two weeks and get some rest and get refocused. He urged us to take a vacation, but we were so broke we just couldn't afford it. But we did take his advice (although it was more of a command) and took a two-week staycation. To be honest with you, most of this staycation was spent sleeping. The rest of it was spent talking with God and with Adessa, trying to sort out everything in my head.

I had to work through all of my worries and fears. I had to face all of my doubts and discouragements. I was honest with God about feelings of dissatisfaction and comparisons I was making between my life and the life of other ministers and pastors. As I poured out my heart to God and eventually Adessa, I began to see that the way I was feeling wasn't legitimate. I began to regain my footing and see God had not left me. He had not abandoned me. Amid the turmoil, grief, and pain of the past year, God was with us the entire time. And I began to see I wasn't alone.

So I understand what Elijah is feeling in this passage. He felt alone, abandoned, and close to death. He couldn't see the forest through the trees, and he was too tired to even look. How did God respond to Elijah?

The Lord said, "Go out and stand on the mountain in the presence of the Lord, for the Lord is about to pass by."

Then a great and powerful wind tore the mountains apart and shattered the rocks before the Lord, but the Lord was not in the wind. After the wind there was an earthquake, but the Lord was not in the earthquake. After the earthquake came a fire, but the Lord was not in the fire. And after the fire came a gentle whisper. When Elijah heard it, he pulled his cloak over his face and went out and stood at the mouth of the cave. - 1 Kings 19:11-13, NIV

God allowed Elijah to experience Him intimately. He saw the power of God exhibited in the wind, earthquake, and fire. Then he experienced the peace of God through a gentle whisper.

Guys, if you find yourself in a place like Elijah, or feeling like I described that I had experienced, it is important for you to get your eyes off the destructive power of the wind, to stop dwelling on the shaking you experience, ignore the heat that your circumstances bring, and find the peace of God. I know that is what I had to do. I had to get my eyes off of everything that left me shaken and focus on the peace of God. Only then could I get to the heart of what needed to be dealt with. This is exactly what happened with Elijah.

Then a voice said to him, "What are you doing here, Elijah?"

He replied, "I have been very zealous for the Lord God Almighty. The Israelites have rejected your covenant, torn down your altars, and put your prophets to death with the sword. I am the only one left, and now they are trying to kill me too." - 1 Kings 19:13-14, NIV

Second verse same as the verse. Elijah gives the exact same answer he gave before. He was scared, exhausted, alone, and feeling like everything he had done for God was a waste. He needed God to minister to him and help him. That is exactly what God did.

> *"Go back the way you came, and go to the Desert of Damascus. When you get there, anoint Hazael king over Aram. Also, anoint Jehu son of Nimshi king over Israel, and anoint Elisha son of Shaphat from Abel Meholah to succeed you as prophet. Jehu will put to death any who escape the sword of Hazael, and Elisha will put to death any who escape the sword of Jehu. Yet I reserve seven thousand in Israel—all whose knees have not bowed down to Baal and whose mouths have not kissed him."*
> *-1 Kings 19:15-18, NIV*

In this passage, I see God giving Elijah three things he desperately needed.

1. God redefined his purpose.

In this passage, God gives Elijah three specific jobs to do. He knows Elijah feels lost and alone, so he gives Elijah a renewed sense of purpose.

The greatest need we have when we feel discouraged is a renewed sense of God's presence in our lives. Nothing says God is still there and willing to help us then God giving us a job to do or a new purpose that we can only do with His help. God is getting Elijah's eyes off of his feelings and back onto his ride or die calling and purpose.

We cannot allow our feelings of discouragement to get us off track and away from God's will for our lives. When discouraged, allow God to refocus your eyes on what He has called you to do. One of the first things I did when I came back from my time off was work on this book. During the two weeks off, God gave me the Mantour theme of *Ignition,* and the theme of this book, *Ride or Die.*

Part of me getting back into my ride or die saddle was working on this book. Allow God to give you a renewed sense of purpose so that you can continue to ride or die in the face of your discouragement.

2. God gave him a friend.

Anoint Elisha son of Shaphat from Abel Meholah to succeed you as prophet. - **1 Kings 19:16**

God knew that Elijah needed someone to ride or die alongside him, so he told him to go and find a dude named Elisha and anoint him as his successor. While this gave Elijah a new purpose, mentoring his replacement, it also gave him a friend. Elijah had been going it alone, and this never works out well. God knew he needed someone alongside him, someone to talk to, to invest in, to share his victories and struggles with as he served God. As he lived a life of riding and dying with God, he and Elisha also rode together.

Allow God to give you a renewed sense of purpose so that you can continue to ride or die in the face of your discouragement.

Guys, you need to have friends in your life. Recently, I saw a stat that left me stunned. It was a men's ministry stat, and it focused on men and friendships. My mouth literally dropped when I read it.

According to the Washington Area Coalition of Men's Ministry,[1] 95% of men say they don't have male friends. The number is slightly better in the church setting. 66% of men who attend church say they don't have other male friends. While that number is better, it is nothing to write home about.

With these numbers, it is no wonder that so many men struggle with feeling alone and isolated. One of the biggest traps I see men of

God fall into is feeling discouraged. They feel they are the only men trying to follow God and live according to His standards. He makes them feel like they shouldn't even bother trying. He gets too many men to abandon their pursuit of riding or dying with God by making them think they are the only one even trying to because it is impossible to do.

God's men need to stop trying to go it alone. There are no Lone Rangers in God's Kingdom. Heck, the Lone Ranger wasn't even alone. He had Tonto! Men, we need each other. We cannot try to go through this thing called life alone and isolated. God calls us to ride and die for Him, but He also calls us to ride and die together.

God calls us to ride and die for Him, but He also calls us to ride and die together.

We see this in the life of Elijah. When feeling discouraged and alone, God gave him a friend to go through life with together. Up until the very end of Elijah's time on earth, we see Elisha refusing to leave his side. Even when Elijah and the other prophets repeatedly tried to get him to stay behind as Elijah went to meet God and leave this earth, he constantly refused, basically saying, *"We will ride or die together until the end!"*

I hope you have such a friend in your life! Are you such a friend? We need to be men who follow this example. How do we do it?

Proverbs tells us exactly how to have friends.

A man who has friends must himself be friendly, But there is a friend who sticks closer than a brother.
-Proverbs 18:24, NKJV

In order to have friends, you have to be friendly to other people. You cannot push people away. You must open yourself up to others and just be a friendly guy. This is how the wisest man in history, Solomon, tells us to have friends…we should probably listen. We must become men who ride or die together with other men of God. That is how we have true success in life. As Clarence Odbody, AS2 (Angel Second Class) writes in the book at the end of *It's a Wonderful Life*, "…Remember no man is a failure who has friends."[3]

3. God gives him hope.

The final thing God did for Elijah to help him overcome his discouragement was to give him hope.

"I reserve seven thousand in Israel—all whose knees have not bowed down to Baal and whose mouths have not kissed him." - 1 Kings 19:18, NIV

One of the biggest sources of discouragement Elijah felt was that he was the only one left trying to follow God. The enemy was whispering in his ear, *"Why are you riding or dying with God? You are the only person left living this way! No one else is even trying. You look like a fool. Just give up and do what makes you happy."*

I see this so often in the lives of men. Heck, I have felt this way! But it is a lie of the enemy used to defeat and discourage God's men. He tries to isolate you and make you feel alone. Reject those lies. There are millions of other men who are living exactly like you are. They get up every day and do their best to love and serve God and obey His word. They faithfully ride or die daily. YOU ARE NOT ALONE!

That is one reason why I started Mantour Conferences over eight years ago, so that men can come to a conference and be surrounded by other men of God. I want men to see they are not alone. Other men are living their daily lives committed to God, riding or dying right beside them for God and His kingdom!

God told Elijah, *"You are not alone. I am with you, and so are 7,000 other men of God who are making the same stand for me as you. Get back out there and do what I called you to do."*

God gave Elijah the hope and strength to ride and die in the face of discouragement. Elijah left Mount Horeb and did what God told him to do. Elijah was not alone, and neither are you!

What about you? Did this chapter help you see how discouragement tries to attack you? Maybe discouragement has already knocked you down, and you're hiding in your cave, unable to get back up. If that's you, I encourage you to get your eyes off of the wind, earthquake, and fire and get it refocussed back on God. Tell Him what has you so discouraged, and allow Him to give you a new purpose. Ask Him to give you a friend to go through life with you, someone you can trust through the good times and the bad. Ask Him to help you see you are not alone. Millions of men are riding and dying along with you. Then get back up and get riding and dying with God with a renewed passion and vigor.

Group Study Questions:

1. How does discouragement affect our ability to ride or die?

2. How can we guard against discouragement after we experience a spiritual victory?

3. How do we get our eyes off of everything that leaves us shaken and get focused on the peace of God? What are some practical ways to do this?

4. Why is it important to have friends? Do you have friends you can rely on in your life?

5. Why is it important to know other men are serving God?

6. After reading this chapter, what is one thing you will put into practice or one thing you will change in your life?

7. How can we, as a group, help you do this?

CHAPTER TEN

RIDE OR DIE THROUGH PERSECUTION

He fell on his knees and cried out, "Lord, do not hold this sin against them."

How many of you have ever received hate mail?

How many have received it from a relative?

If I was asked that question, I'd have to raise my hand and say, *"ME!"*

It was a few years ago when Adessa and I had just started ministering. Back in those early days, much of our ministry focused on sharing our testimony of how God revealed my Dad's family secrets to us, showed us how they affected our lives, and healed us from the damage these secrets created in our lives. Many heard our testimony and were encouraged to seek God's healing in their own lives. However, one of our relatives was less than thrilled.

Instead, she'd somehow heard what we were teaching and sent us a nasty letter telling us how much she hated what we were doing. It was the first time we'd ever received hate mail, but it wasn't the last time we would be persecuted by family members who didn't like what we were preaching.

Even today, there are still many family members who will not speak to us. We can drive past them in the car, and they won't even wave back (we always try to wave at them). Strangely, they will talk to our dad, but they don't want anything to do with the crazy Jesus freaks who've turned into traveling preachers.

Unfortunately, our story is all too common.

Today, we live in a world where Christians are starting to face animosity and hatred just for living out our beliefs.

We are mocked in Hollywood. Many news outlets call us *"right wing extremists."* The other day I was reading an article where a popular Christian was berated for being a hateful *"fundamentalist"* (trust me, they used *"fundamentalist"* as a dirty word) simply because they held to the Biblical view of marriage.

We no longer live in a country that embraces Christianity. Many believers are starting to see this carry over into their personal lives. This leaves us with the question of *"how do we respond to people who hate us for our Christian beliefs?"*

What do you do when a parent says they don't want your child playing with their child because your child told them about Jesus?

How do you respond when you are told you must compromise your personal convictions in order to keep your job?

What do you do when your friends or family abandon you because of your faith?

How do we ride or die for our faith and still show people the love of Jesus?

In the book of Acts, Stephen sets an example we can all follow when we are in this situation.

Let's take a look at his story:

> *Now Stephen, a man full of God's grace and power, performed great wonders and signs among the people. Opposition arose, however, from members of the Synagogue of the Freedmen (as it was called)—Jews of Cyrene and Alexandria as well as the provinces of Cilicia and Asia—who began to argue with Stephen. But they could not stand up against the wisdom the Spirit gave him as he spoke.*
>
> *Then they secretly persuaded some men to say, "We have heard Stephen speak blasphemous words against Moses and against God."*
>
> *So they stirred up the people and the elders and the teachers of the law. They seized Stephen and brought him before the Sanhedrin. They produced false witnesses, who testified, "This fellow never stops speaking against this holy place and against the law. For we have heard him say that this Jesus of Nazareth will destroy this place and change the customs Moses handed down to us."* - **Acts 6:8-14, NIV**

Even though he had done nothing wrong, Stephen was in deep trouble because men who hated him had lied about him and brought him before the courts.

Knowing he faced possible imprisonment or even death, Stephen had some choices to make.

He could back down and apologize for "*offending*" the Jews for his intolerance or the message that offended them and try to save his own skin. Or he could speak the truth and take the consequences.

This couldn't have been an easy decision, and yet, filled with the Holy Spirit, Stephen stood firm, spoke the truth, and preached the Gospel Message (including the parts they didn't want to hear) to the crowd.

> *Then the high priest asked Stephen, "Are these charges true?" To this he replied: "Brothers and fathers, listen to me! The God of glory appeared to our father Abraham while he was still in Mesopotamia, before he lived in Harran. 'Leave your country and your people,' God said, 'and go to the land I will show you.'*
>
> *So he left the land of the Chaldeans and settled in Harran. After the death of his father, God sent him to this land where you are now living. He gave him no inheritance here, not even enough ground to set his foot on. But God promised him that he and his descendants after him would possess the land, even though at that time Abraham had no child." - Acts 7:1-5, NIV*

Stephen had his chance to defend himself. Over the next forty-eight verses, Stephen retold all of Israel's history from Abraham to the present and showed how Jesus was the fulfillment of all the law and prophets. He told them how God's plan throughout history was fulfilled by Jesus. He then tells them that, just as Israel had done throughout history, they, too, didn't want to hear the truth. Israel constantly rejected the prophets, and they rejected the final prophet who fulfilled all prophecies, Jesus. He calls them out for crucifying

Jesus because of their rebellious hearts. He spoke the truth to them in love, not backing down from what was right.

If this were Hollywood, Stephen would have persuaded the people with his words, and there would have been a huge revival. That's not what happened. (Because the Bible is real.)

Instead, the Jewish leaders became enraged, dragged him out of the city, and began stoning him.

This is where Stephen's ride or die character came shining through.

Instead of fighting them, responding in anger, or even calling down curses on them, Stephen followed Jesus' example and said, "*Lord, don't charge them with this sin!*"

And then he died.

In all of his actions, he set an example for us to follow.

1. We must speak the truth in love.

Stephen knew the Pharisees and leaders were living in rebellion against God. They had become cold and hard-hearted to the ways of God. They legalistically obeyed the rules, but they didn't love God or genuinely serve Him. If they had, they would have seen Jesus had fulfilled all the prophecies and laws they were fighting to maintain. Instead of responding to the will and direction of God that challenged them spiritually, they crucified Jesus.

Stephen understood this and tried one more time to point their sin out in love. He spoke the truth, hoping to break through their hard hearts. He wanted them to come to Christ and truly serve God, not ritualistic worship.

You see, it's hard for us, as Americans, with our fight-to-win attitude to understand that as followers of Jesus, we are called to do both: stand for truth and love our enemies. Remember, love doesn't lie to people. We need to follow Stephen's example and continue speaking and standing for Biblical truth in a loving way in hopes that those who hear will repent and come into a personal relationship with God.

Still, don't expect your truth to be popular. It will probably bring the Twitter mob and those who don't agree against us, but we need to ride or die in love and continue to speak the truth.

2. We must depend on God for help.

While they were stoning him, Stephen prayed, "Lord Jesus, receive my spirit." - Acts 7:59, NIV

Stephen was drug out of the city and stoned to death. This is so against our Hollywood-trained minds where the Avengers always win, and the Justice League never dies. But in real life, people die every day for their faith. We haven't seen it happen in America yet, but I do believe it is coming. You can see it coming in the distance as the world hates us for speaking the truth, and Progressive Christians try to straddle both sides of the line but never really stand for God. True believers will face persecution.

I am writing this chapter just days after our President withdrew all troops from Afghanistan, handing control of the country over to the terrorists known as the Taliban. For twenty years, Afghanistan lived under freedom. Women didn't have to wear burkas. They were allowed to go to school and have careers. The entire country had experienced freedom. The average age of an Afghanistan citizen is twenty-five years old, which means a majority of them have only known freedom. Now they are back under Taliban control.

Even as I write this chapter, Christians in Afghanistan are being killed for their faith. The Taliban is going door-to-door, hunting and killing Christians. I saw a post on Facebook of a Christian asking people to pray for them to have the boldness to stand for Jesus even if they are killed for it. She asked for prayers for her children to not deny God but to stand strong. The post ended with the statement that they were now gone. They had been killed for their faith.

Heartbreaking isn't a strong enough word for this. But they loved God, they had a ride or die attitude, and in their moment of death, they chose to stand with God and not deny Him. They depended on God for help, and He gave them the strength they needed.

In their moment of death, they chose to stand with God and not deny Him. They depended on God for help, and He gave them the strength they needed.

I can't help but ask myself, *"Would I be able to do the same?"* Would I be strong enough to stand faithful, to ride or die with God in love? Would God give me what I needed to do this?

Mark 13:11 says:

> **Whenever you are arrested and brought to trial, do not worry beforehand about what to say. Just say whatever is given you at the time, for it is not you speaking, but the Holy Spirit. (NIV)**

This passage says that when we ride or die for God during persecution, He will ride or die with us. The Holy Spirit will give us the strength to stand if we are wholeheartedly devoted to Him. That woman and her children in Afghanistan received what they needed to stand firm, even through martyrdom. Stephen did as well, and we will, too.

3. We must show God's love and forgiveness to those who attack us.

How can we show them love and forgiveness? Like the people Jesus spoke to in Matthew 5:43-48, we often see people as *'for us'* or *'against us.'* We're tempted to love those who are for us while showing our angry, antagonistic side to those who disagree. Jesus said this is wrong. Instead, He said we should, ***"Love your enemies! Pray for those who persecute you!" - Matthew 5:44, NIV***

That's the answer to the question: We are called to do both! It's what Stephen did.

Moments away from death for riding and dying with God, Stephen uttered some of the most magnificent words possible. On death's door, he found the courage and strength to pray a prayer of love and forgiveness for His persecutors.

> *While they were stoning him, Stephen prayed, "Lord Jesus, receive my spirit." Then he fell on his knees and cried out, "Lord, do not hold this sin against them." When he had said this, he fell asleep. - Acts 7:59-60, NIV*

Stephen found the strength to pray to God for His persecutors. He spoke words of love and forgiveness. What a ride or die man of God! Like Jesus on the cross, he forgave those who killed him. His love for God outshone any anger or passion for revenge. He didn't ask for a lightning bolt to kill them. He didn't ask for angels to fight against them and rescue him. Instead, he chose to ride and die in love and forgiveness.

Like Stephen, we must stand for the truth while showing Christlike love at the same time. This is so hard. When I experience persecution, I want to fight back. I want revenge. I want them to suffer for the wrong they are doing.

I'll be honest and say that when I received that hateful letter in the mail, I didn't want to just laugh it off and pray. I wanted to whip a few choice words back at her. But I didn't because that's not what Jesus calls us to do. When experiencing persecution, we need to respond as Jesus would. If we are suffering for Him, then we need to respond like Him.

Jesus tells us to love our enemies. We must pray for them. It isn't easy, but it's part of being a ride or die follower of Christ. We aren't called to be defensive or go into counterattack mode. We are called to ride or die in love and forgiveness.

> Jesus tells us to love our enemies. We must pray for them. It isn't easy, but it's part of being a ride or die follower of Christ.

Stephen shines bright as an example of how to ride or die through persecution. We need to all choose to lay down our weapons and start using the things God told us to use: prayer and forgiveness. We need to speak Biblical truth in love. Refuse to take revenge or fight the same way they do. Instead, we need to show love, mercy, and forgiveness as we stand for truth. It's not an either/or choice between truth and love. A ride or die man of God needs to stand for truth in love, and if need be, be willing to die for it.

Group Study Questions:

1. How are Christians in America experiencing persecution today?

2. How are we suppose to handle it when the world persecutes us?

3. Why is it important to show love and forgiveness to those who persecute us?

4. This goes against our natural tendencies. How do we practically do it?

5. After reading this chapter, what is one thing you will put into practice or one thing you will change in your life?

6. How can we, as a group, help you do this?

CHAPTER ELEVEN

RIDE OR DIE FOR GOD'S WORD

The king stood by the pillar and renewed the covenant in the presence of the Lord—to follow the Lord and keep his commands, statutes and decrees with all his heart and all his soul, thus confirming the words of the covenant written in this book.

Have you ever received a Christmas present in May? How about a birthday present seven months after your birthday? Maybe Easter chocolate in November? If you can say *"yes"* to any of this, then you, too, probably had a relative who frequently forgot where they hid a present.

My grandmother was notorious for this. Almost every year during her spring cleaning, she would come across a gift or present she had hidden and forgotten about. It was pretty funny!

We all do this periodically. Recently, Adessa was looking for a suitcase to use for a ministry trip. She found one and, when she opened it, was pleasantly surprised to find it filled with winter clothes. I ran out of drawer space and had stored these sweaters that I rarely wear (I'm a big dude, sweaters make me sweat!) in the suitcase and forgotten all about them.

One time Adessa hit it big while spring cleaning. She found a box of her favorite chocolate that she hid so everyone else didn't eat it. It had been there for a few years!

We all tend to hide stuff and forget where it is hidden sometime in our lives. Usually, it isn't a huge deal. However, sometimes we hide things of great value like a key or important documents, and when the time comes to need them, we panic when we can't find them.

In this chapter, we are going to read about a man who found himself in an awful spot. He and his people found something that NEVER should have been lost. However, his reaction to this should inspire us all today. Let's look at what King Josiah found and how he handled it.

King Josiah became king of Judah at the age of eight! That is so young to be made king! His grandfather, Manasseh, was the worst king in Judah's history. Manasseh was a violent, horrible king who destroyed the worship of God, killed the prophet Isaiah, and introduced Judah to the most horrendous idolatry they could ever experience. Blood flowed in the streets from Manasseh's cruelty. However, Manasseh eventually repented and returned to God. He lived out his final days serving God and obeying him.

After his death, Manasseh's son took the throne. King Amon decided to follow the ways of young Manasseh. As a result, he was assassinated. This is why young Josiah was thrust to the throne at the age of eight.

Josiah never knew his grandfather's evil ways. He only knew Manasseh post-conversion. He followed the path of the repentant Manasseh and served God wholeheartedly.

> *Josiah was eight years old when he became king, and he reigned in Jerusalem thirty-one years.... He did what was right in the eyes of the Lord and followed completely the ways of his father David, not turning aside to the right or to the left.*

> *In the eighteenth year of his reign, King Josiah sent the secretary, Shaphan son of Azaliah, the son of Meshullam, to the temple of the Lord. He said: "Go up to Hilkiah the high priest and have him get ready the money that has been brought into the temple of the Lord, which the doorkeepers have collected from the people. Have them entrust it to the men appointed to supervise the work on the temple. And have these men pay the workers who repair the temple of the Lord— the carpenters, the builders and the masons. Also have them purchase timber and dressed stone to repair the temple. But they need not account for the money entrusted to them, because they are honest in their dealings." - 2 Kings 22:1-7, NIV*

Josiah decided God's temple had been neglected long enough. He decided it was time to repair it to its former glory, showing the people that the worship of God was paramount to his kingdom.

As the men began the work on the temple, they found something that had been hidden and forgotten about.

> *Hilkiah the high priest said to Shaphan the secretary, "I have found the Book of the Law in the temple of the Lord."*

> *He gave it to Shaphan, who read it. Then Shaphan the secretary went to the king and reported to him: "Your officials have paid out the money that was in the temple of the Lord and have entrusted it to the workers and supervisors at the temple." Then Shaphan the secretary informed the king, "Hilkiah the priest has given me a book." And Shaphan read from it in the presence of the king. - 2 Kings 22:8-10, NIV*

Judah had actually lost the Word of God! The Bible as they knew it at that time was so neglected that it got hidden and lost! How was this possible? How did God's people lose God's Word!

They had fallen into so much idolatry and sin that they didn't even bother consulting the Bible on how to live. This is so heartbreaking, yet it is easy to understand.

Unfortunately, believers do it all the time. Just look at this stat. Between early 2019 and 2020, the percentage of US adults who say they use the Bible daily dropped from 14% to 9%, according to the State of the Bible 2020 report released by the Barna Group and the American Bible Society.[1] Only 14% of people said they read God's Word daily, pre-pandemic. That is so sad! But it is even worse since the Covid-19 pandemic. Now only 9% read God's Word daily.

The numbers are equally pathetic for believers. A Lifeway Research survey in 2019 found that only 32% of Protestant Christians read the Bible daily. 27% read it a few times a week, 12% once a week, and 5% once a month. 12% of Protestant Christians say they never read God's Word! [2]

Those are pitiful numbers for both Christians as well as a nation that claims to be *"One nation, under God."* We need to break this trend immediately. We need to make sure we haven't hidden God's

Word away and forgotten all about it as Judah did. We need to understand a few things.

1. Christian men MUST read God's Word.

Honestly, it is impossible to live as a strong Christian if you are not reading God's Word. I didn't say you have to read the Bible to be a Christian. Salvation comes through faith in Jesus, no other way. But to be a strong Christian, you must read God's Word. Otherwise, we stay weak and defeated. Why?

The words in the Bible help us when we face our enemy. When we know what the Bible says, and we function in the power of the Holy Spirit, we have the spiritual strength of Captain America. Nothing can defeat us. We are invincible. When the enemy fights us, we can fight confidently and say to him Cap's famous line, "*I can do this all day.*"[3]

It is impossible to live as a strong Christian if you are not reading God's word.

Unfortunately, too many of God's children don't read God's Word, and instead of being a stud like Captain America, they are instead weak-kneed Barney Fife from the Andy Griffith show, running around with one bullet in our pocket, and losing the fight before it even starts.

This is why we created our year-long Bible reading plans for men. Our 2022 Bible plan is also themed "*Ride or Die.*" It contains daily Bible reading passages and a weekly devotional. In 2022, the devotionals are being written not just by me, but my friends and ministry partners, who also believe in the need for God's men to read the word. In 2022, you can get it emailed to you daily for free or buy a print copy to have a physical copy of the plan. More information is available at mantourministries.com/Bibleplan.

Christian men must read God's Word. It is how we gain the power to win against the enemy's attacks. Jesus knew this. He fought the temptations of Satan by quoting the Word of God to defeat him. The enemy can't fight against truth, and God's Word, which is absolute truth, exposes the enemy for what he is: the father of lies. To be a strong man of God, you must read God's Word. However, reading the Bible isn't enough. This brings us to point two.

2. Godly men are convicted by God's Word.

> *When the king heard the words of the Book of the Law, he tore his robes. He gave these orders to Hilkiah the priest, Ahikam son of Shaphan, Akbor son of Micaiah, Shaphan the secretary and Asaiah the king's attendant: "Go and inquire of the Lord for me and for the people and for all Judah about what is written in this book that has been found. Great is the Lord's anger that burns against us because those who have gone before us have not obeyed the words of this book; they have not acted in accordance with all that is written there concerning us." - 2 Kings 22:11-13, NIV*

Hearing God's Word wrecked him. He was brought to tears and tore his robe seeing how far God's people were living from God's ways.

Josiah immediately recognized that the entire nation had sinned against God. They had ceased to follow and obey God's Word. Immediately, he was convicted for the sins he and Judah had committed against God.

Guys, we need to allow the Word of God to convict us. The Bible is God's Holy Word. We are unholy, sinful men. So every time we read the Word, it should help us see areas in our life we can make changes. God's Word shines a light into the dark places inside of us. This light should show us areas we need to change. Repentance should always be a result of reading God's Word. This allows God's Word to change us and make us more like Jesus. As a result, we should make changes, which brings us to point three.

Repentance should always be a result of reading God's word. This allows God's word to change us and make us more like Jesus.

3. A ride or die man of God takes action after reading God's Word.

Josiah was devastated after hearing God's Word. He knew they had sinned against God, and action needed to be taken. So he sent for the prophetess, who basically said, *"I'm sorry, but it's too late. God is going to judge His people for their sins. But it won't happen in your lifetime."*

At this point, Josiah could have done a few things. He could have seen the situation as hopeless and thought, *"Nothing I can do."* He could have taken a deep breath and said, *"At least it won't happen to me."*

Instead, he decided to ride or die with God's Word! Josiah rolled up his sleeves and got to work getting rid of ALL idols and every single thing associated with idol worship in his kingdom. Josiah became EXTREME—getting rid of EVERY SINGLE THING that was against God's Law.

> *The king ordered Hilkiah the high priest, the priests next in rank and the doorkeepers to remove from the temple of the*

Lord all the articles made for Baal and Asherah and all the starry hosts. He burned them outside Jerusalem in the fields of the Kidron Valley and took the ashes to Bethel. He did away with the idolatrous priests appointed by the kings of Judah to burn incense on the high places of the towns of Judah and on those around Jerusalem—those who burned incense to Baal, to the sun and moon, to the constellations and to all the starry hosts. He took the Asherah pole from the temple of the Lord to the Kidron Valley outside Jerusalem and burned it there. He ground it to powder and scattered the dust over the graves of the common people. He also tore down the quarters of the male shrine prostitutes that were in the temple of the Lord, the quarters where women did weaving for Asherah.

Josiah brought all the priests from the towns of Judah and desecrated the high places, from Geba to Beersheba, where the priests had burned incense. He broke down the gateway at the entrance of the Gate of Joshua, the city governor, which was on the left of the city gate. Although the priests of the high places did not serve at the altar of the Lord in Jerusalem, they ate unleavened bread with their fellow priests.

He desecrated Topheth, which was in the Valley of Ben Hinnom, so no one could use it to sacrifice their son or daughter in the fire to Molek. He removed from the entrance to the temple of the Lord the horses that the kings of Judah had dedicated to the sun. They were in the court near the room of an official named Nathan-Melek. Josiah then burned the chariots dedicated to the sun.

He pulled down the altars the kings of Judah had erected on the roof near the upper room of Ahaz, and the altars

Manasseh had built in the two courts of the temple of the Lord. He removed them from there, smashed them to pieces and threw the rubble into the Kidron Valley. The king also desecrated the high places that were east of Jerusalem on the south of the Hill of Corruption—the ones Solomon king of Israel had built for Ashtoreth the vile goddess of the Sidonians, for Chemosh the vile god of Moab, and for Molek the detestable god of the people of Ammon. Josiah smashed the sacred stones and cut down the Asherah poles and covered the sites with human bones.

Even the altar at Bethel, the high place made by Jeroboam son of Nebat, who had caused Israel to sin—even that altar and high place he demolished. He burned the high place and ground it to powder, and burned the Asherah pole also.
- 2 Kings 23:4-15, NIV

Josiah took decisive action...but he didn't stop there!

Just as he had done at Bethel, Josiah removed all the shrines at the high places that the kings of Israel had built in the towns of Samaria and that had aroused the Lord's anger. Josiah slaughtered all the priests of those high places on the altars and burned human bones on them. Then he went back to Jerusalem.

The king gave this order to all the people: "Celebrate the Passover to the Lord your God, as it is written in this Book of the Covenant." Neither in the days of the judges who led Israel nor in the days of the kings of Israel and the kings of Judah had any such Passover been observed. But in the eighteenth year of King Josiah, this Passover was celebrated to the Lord in Jerusalem.

> *Furthermore, Josiah got rid of the mediums and spiritists, the household gods, the idols and all the other detestable things seen in Judah and Jerusalem. This he did to fulfill the requirements of the law written in the book that Hilkiah the priest had discovered in the temple of the Lord. Neither before nor after Josiah was there a king like him who turned to the Lord as he did—with all his heart and with all his soul and with all his strength, in accordance with all the Law of Moses. - 2 Kings 23:19-25, NIV*

Josiah didn't follow just a little—no, he was EXTREME in his obedience.

Why? Because he knew that up until then, his people were EXTREME in their disobedience.

Then, he got God's Temple back in shape and re-instituted the proper practices for worshiping God that had been abandoned long ago. He led the people in celebrating the Passover and did all that he could to get the people back on track.

Josiah was a true ride or die man of God's Word. He read it, repented, and then moved forward in obedience. 2 Kings 23:25 describes him this way: *"Neither before nor after Josiah was there a king like him who turned to the Lord as he did—with all his heart and with all his soul and with all his strength, in accordance with all the Law of Moses."*

Today, King Josiah sets an example that many of us need to follow as we commit to being ride or die men of God.

I remember a time in my life where we had to have a Josiah day. I had a grandfather who, for lack of a better term, was a thief. I don't think there was any gift he gave me that wasn't stolen. He stole so much stuff from his place of work. Being completely honest, we never realized most of what he gave us was stolen. But then, one Sunday, we heard a sermon on this very passage we are reading in this chapter, and as a family, we realized we needed to clean house and get rid of everything he had ever given us so that we were not holding on to stolen goods.

We searched every room, every closet, every corner of the basement and found everything he had given us. There was so much stolen stuff that we had to rent two dumpsters to get rid of it all! But God's Word had convicted us as a family, and we took extreme action and cleaned the house.

I remember another time where the Holy Spirit convicted me for how much of an idol I had made of the game of golf. Because of my disability, golf was the only sport I was ever able to play really well. As a result, I made golf too much of an idol in my life. In order to get the victory, I went extreme and threw away everything I had related to golf. It was hard, but God's conviction showed me I had to take action.

There have been times when God's Word convicted me of tv shows I was watching, friendships I was entertaining, books I was reading, and so much more. I had to get rid of them from my life immediately!

We need to stop making excuses for our sin and compromise and go to extremes in passionate obedience to God.

Guys, it is time for us to go through our lives, through our hearts, maybe even through our houses, and get rid of everything that doesn't please God. It's time for us to stop saying, *"Well, everyone else is doing it. No one else has a problem with it."* We need to stop making excuses for our sin and compromise and go to extremes in passionate obedience to God.

It's time to get rid of books, magazines, internet sites, television shows, movies, hobbies, habits, or anything else that is displeasing to God. We need to abandon anything that is connected with the occult, magic, witchcraft, yoga, or any foreign religion. It's time we stopped playing around with pornography and say, *"Once and for all, it's out of here."* It could be alcohol or an especially violent video game. Really, the possibilities are endless of sinful things that Christians entertain that should be abolished from their lives.

It's time to go all Josiah on these things and get them out of our lives once and for all!

Then we need to commit to ride or die, implementing true spiritual disciplines into our lives. We need a fresh commitment to prayer, Bible reading, and Bible study.

It's time to make a ride or die commitment to obeying God and abandoning disobedience. It's time for a Josiah day. If we are to be true ride or die men of God, we must not just read God's Word but also allow it to convict us and then act on this conviction and make changes. It is time to allow God's Word to have a life-changing impact on our lives. Like Josiah, our entire legacy can become one of being a ride or die man of God's Word. I can't think of a better legacy for a man of God!

Group Study Questions:

1. Be honest: How often do you read the Bible?

2. This chapter states: *"It is impossible to live as a strong Christian if you are not reading God's Word."* Do you agree with this? Why or why not?

3. What was the last thing you felt convicted of while reading the Bible? Did you repent and make a change?

4. Josiah was EXTREME in his obedience. What action can you take to be EXTREME in your obedience to God's Word?

5. Will you commit to reading God's Word daily? (You should take advantage of Mantour Ministries Year-Long Bible Plan, available in print format as well as a free email format.)

6. After reading this chapter, what is one thing you will put into practice or one thing you will change in your life?

7. How can we, as a group, help you do this?

CONCLUSION

I could go on and on, but I've run out of time. There are so many more—
Gideon, Barak, Samson, Jephthah, David, Samuel, the prophets. ... Through
acts of faith, they toppled kingdoms, made justice work, took the promises for
themselves. They were protected from lions, fires, and sword thrusts, turned
disadvantage to advantage, won battles, routed alien armies. Women received
their loved ones back from the dead. There were those who, under torture,
refused to give in and go free, preferring something better: resurrection. Others
braved abuse and whips, and, yes, chains and dungeons. We have stories of those
who were stoned, sawed in two, murdered in cold blood; stories of vagrants
wandering the earth in animal skins, homeless, friendless, powerless—the world
didn't deserve them!—making their way as best they could on the cruel edges of
the world.

We have reached the end of our time together in this book. We
have looked at some of the greatest men in the Bible who, when faced

with life's tough decisions and situations, chose to ride and die with God.

- Noah was a man who chose to ride and die obediently.

- Thomas demonstrated to us that our personality or past struggles do not define us. We can overcome and ride or die with God.

- Peter chose to ride and die with all of his heart.

- Nehemiah chose to ride or die to fulfill his God-given purpose.

- Abraham proved his decision to ride or die with God was not based on what he could get out of the deal, but simply because he loved God.

- Daniel was able to ride or die because he had the resolve to do whatever was necessary to follow God, no matter what others thought or said.

- Shadrach, Meshack, and Abednego showed no matter what they faced or even how God responded, they would ride or die.

- Elijah is a shining example of choosing to ride or die in the face of discouragement.

- Stephen showed us how to ride or die in the face of persecution.

- Josiah showed us how to ride or die with God's Word, allowing it to impact our lives and cause us to make changes.

Every one of these men of God was an ordinary man just like you and me. But their decision to ride or die for God raised them from the status of ordinary guys to extraordinary living legends in God's Kingdom. Just like us, they faced trials, struggles, temptations, and tendencies that had the potential to destroy their walk with God. But each of them stood through the tests and became the men we look up to and pattern our spiritual journeys after.

These are just some of the stories in the Bible of men and women who daily chose to ride and die with God. Hebrews 11, which we started this chapter with, says what could easily be said about this book. I don't have time to tell you about every man and woman of God in the Bible and throughout history who has made that decision that, no matter what, I will ride or die with God!

We looked at ten men in this book, and our accompanying Bible reading plan, *"Ride or Die, a Year-Long Bible Plan,"* shares 52 devotionals about men who made similar choices throughout history to ride or die with reckless abandon for God. I could fill volumes of books telling the stories of men and women who have made this choice to ride or die. History is full of them. You know what, you could also join their ranks as you decide to ride or die with God!

I hope this book has inspired you to make the choices they made, that no matter what they encountered, what trials they faced, or whatever God required of them, they would ride or die with Him!

As you daily choose to live with a ride or die attitude, you could be the legend future generations admire.

As you daily choose to live with a ride or die attitude, you could be the legend future generations admire.

You see, that is really what it is all about. Their choice to ride and die with God inspires us to follow their example, and we need to do the same for the next generation.

We have a world of young men and women out there growing up without a strong, Christ-like male role model. We can be a living example to them of how to walk with God, surrender completely to Him, and trust Him no matter what. They can learn from us how to hear God's voice and respond to His call. They can see us hear God's challenge and watch us fist-pump God and say, *"No matter what, I will ride and die with You!"* and be inspired to do the same.

So I end this book with the same questions I asked earlier. Has this book challenged you that, no matter what you are going through, you will choose to have a ride or die attitude with God?

Will you decide that there is nothing God could ask of you that you would not be willing to do?

If it means you will go to the ends of the earth for God and taking risks for Him, will you stand by Him and for Him no matter the cost? Will you ride with Him even if it ends up killing you?

I want to end this book with the same challenge we started out asking. Will you make a statement of extreme loyalty and devotion to God, no matter what He does, where He leads, or what He asks of you?

Will you ride or die with God? I have chosen to answer, *"I will ride or die with God, no matter what!"* What will you decide?

Group Study Questions:

1. After reading through this book, what does the phrase *Ride or Die* now mean to you?

2. How will your decision to ride or die affect future generations?

3. Will you decide that there is nothing God could ask of you that you would not be willing to do?

4. If it means you will go to the ends of the earth for God and taking risks for Him, will you stand by Him and for Him no matter the cost?

5. Will you ride with Him even if it ends up killing you?

6. Will you make a statement of extreme loyalty and devotion to God, no matter what He does, where He leads, or what He asks of you?

WORKBOOK

Chapter One:

-As God's son's, we need to be saying to Him in the dark, difficult times, "I'm still _____ to you. I will _____ you through the good times, and even the bad. I will _____ or _____ with you!"

-When the going gets_____, will you _____ _____?

What does the thought of "Ride or Die" spiritually cause you to feel? Write it down below:

Group Study Questions:

1. What does the phrase, *"Ride or Die"* mean spiritually?

2. This chapter stated, *"To spiritually ride or die means we have to pick up our cross for Jesus."* What is your reaction to this statement?

3. What is your greatest fear when it comes to picking up your cross and following Jesus?

4. Is this fear rational? Or would it not be as bad as you think?

5. After reading this chapter, what is one thing you will put into practice or one thing you will change in your life?

6. How can we, as a group, help you do this?

Chapter 2:

-Even when everyone around him pursued _____ and _____, Noah determined to ride or die with God!

-God knew that whatever He asked of Noah, Noah would fist pump Him and say, "I'm riding or dying with you..._____ _____ _____!"

-One generations obedience leads to the _____ _____ _____.

What is an area of your life that you have struggled to obey God?

Write down three steps you can take to begin walking in obedience in this area.

1.

2.

3.

Group Study Questions:

1. Why did God choose Noah to build the ark?

2. Has God ever asked you to do something that, to you, made absolutely no sense? Did you do it? What was the result?

3. This chapter made the point: *"Obedience brings the big job; the big job doesn't bring obedience."* What does this mean to you?

4. Are there any times where you don't respond properly when God asks you to do something? What changes do you need to make?

5. How can your obedience or disobedience affect your children?

6. After reading this chapter, what is one thing you will put into practice or one thing you will change in your life?

7. How can we, as a group, help you do this?

Chapter Three

-There is no such things as _____ zones in God's kingdom. There is just obedience and following, no _____ _____.

-The same power that raised Jesus from the dead lives in you and this power can help you overcome your natural _____ or _____.

What is an area where you struggle to overcome because of your natural personality?

What is the hardest thing for you to do as a Christian? I.e. witness, trust, surrender

What steps can you take to overcome your personality or weakness and boldly ride or die?

1.

2.

3.

Group Study Questions:

1. Did you have a nickname growing up? Was it a positive or negative nickname? How did it affect you?

2. Thomas shows us it is possible to overcome our personalities and boldly follow Jesus. What area of your life or personality keeps you from riding or dying with God?

3. This chapter states: *"There are no such things as comfort zones in God's kingdom. There is just obedience and following, no highway option."* How does this statement make you feel?

4. What area of your life do you feel the most timid?

5. How can you overcome this timidity and move for with a ride or die attitude?

6. After reading this chapter, what is one thing you will put into practice or one thing you will change in your life?

7. How can we, as a group, help you do this?

Chapter 4:

-Salvation and eternal life only come through _____
our needs, turning to God for _____ of our
sins, and_____ our lives to ride or die as God's
servant.

-In order to reach our full potential as God's man, we must be willing
to _____ _____ _____.

What area of sin in your life keeps you from wholeheartedly
surrendering to God? Write it down.

Write down three actions you will take to overcome in this area:

1.

2.

3.

RIDE OR DIE

Group Study Questions:

1. The rich young ruler had the wrong idea of what it takes to follow God. How would you define what it takes to follow God?

2. The rich young ruler wouldn't surrender everything to God. Is there anything that you struggle to submit that is keeping you from riding or dying with God?

3. Why do you think Peter could surrender and follow God wholeheartedly, but the rich young ruler couldn't?

4. What are you willing to give up for God?

5. What are you willing to separate yourself from for Him?

6. Will you ride or die with Him with your whole heart, soul, mind, and being, holding nothing back?

7. After reading this chapter, what is one thing you will put into practice or one thing you will change in your life?

8. How can we, as a group, help you do this?

Chapter 5

-Your purpose isn't always a call to full-time ministry, but its always to do something with your _____ and _____ that needs to be done to _____ _____'s kingdom.

-When _____ and resistance to your purpose comes against you, you need to follow Nehemiah's example, drop to you knees, ask God for _____ and victory, and continue to _____ the _____ .

-You do not know what _____ _____ your ride or die decision to fulfill your God-given purpose will have on others.

Have you discovered your true purpose in life? Write it down below:

What is the biggest obstacle keeping you from fulfilling your purpose?

Write down three ways you can conquer this obstacle.

1.

2.

3.

Group Study Questions:

1. What does it mean to find your purpose?

2. How do we respond when we face resistance from the enemy and others as we pursue our purpose?

3. In this chapter, we stated, *"You do not know what eternal consequences your ride or die decision to fulfill your God-given purpose will have on others."* What does this mean? How does it challenge you to fulfill your purpose?

4. What is the biggest obstacle keeping you from fulfilling your purpose?

5. What can you do to overcome this obstacle?

6. After reading this chapter, what is one thing you will put into practice or one thing you will change in your life?

7. How can we, as a group, help you do this?

Chapter 6

-Do we ride or die for God because of what we can _____ _____ of it, or do we do it simply because _____ _____ us to?

-Do you ride or die because of what God _____ you or because you _____ Him?

-God still requires His men to ride or die with Him, not just to get what they can out of the deal, but simply because they _____ Him, _____ Him, and are _____ to Him above all else.

What is God asking you to sacrifice for Him?

What is keeping you from obeying?

Write down three actions you can take to sacrifice this area to God.

1.

2.

3.

Group Study Questions:

1. This chapter asked the question: *"Do we ride or die for God because of what we can get out of it, or do we do it simply because He asks us to?"* What is your honest answer?

2. Is serving God and following Him simply because He asked you enough reason for you to ride or die for Him?

3. Are you willing to ride or die with God even if it means that He doesn't take you on the road you expected to go on?

4. What if He asks you to sacrifice your dreams to Him? Will you do it?

5. What if He asks you to give up the things in your life that you think are important but He sees as distractions or hindrances? Will you obey?

6. After reading this chapter, what is one thing you will put into practice or one thing you will change in your life?

7. How can we, as a group, help you do this?

Chapter 7

-Everywhere Daniel went, his commitment to _____ and _____ God went with him.

-When the world says, "You can't _____ that" or "You can't _____ that", will you submit to mob culture, or do it _____'s ways.

-You will not win any _____ cookies from the world or from Progressive Christianity for standing _____ for what you know to be true, but God will always _____ your choice.

Are there any areas of your life where you have compromised what you believe to gain acceptance of others? Make a list of ways below:

Write down a prayer of repentance below:

What are some steps you can take to get back on track and stand for God's ways?

1.

2.

3.

Group Study Questions:

1. This chapter stated: *"Everywhere Daniel went, his commitment to follow and obey God went with him."* Can you say the same about yourself?

2. Daniel had people try and tell him how to serve God? How do you see this happening today?

3. What is the danger of Progressive Christianity? How can you avoid its trap and help others do the same?

4. When the world says, *"You can't say that"* or *"You can't do that,"* will you submit to mob culture, or do it God's ways, no matter the results?

5. Will you resolve today to serve and obey God even if it goes against the culture and even if it causes persecution?

6. After reading this chapter, what is one thing you will put into practice or one thing you will change in your life?

7. How can we, as a group, help you do this?

Chapter 8

-We need to search our hearts and see if there is even a hint of participating in foreign _____ or _____ worship in our lives.

-Even if God doesn't come through, make the choice _____ _____ _____.

-Riding or dying in faith could cost you everything here on earth, but God will never _____ you or _____ you.

Write down any ways you have allowed idol worship into your life:

Write down two actions you can take to remove these idols:

1.

2.

Group Study Questions:

1. Are you allowing any foreign religions or idols in your life? If so, will you commit to removing them?

2. Shadrach, Meshack, and Abednego committed to obey God even if God didn't come through for them. Will you make the same choice not to bow even if God doesn't come through and do what you want?

3. This chapter stated: *"Riding or dying in faith could cost you everything here on earth, but God will never leave you or forsake you."* What does this mean to you?

4. What scares you most about riding or dying in faith?

5. Is it a rational fear? Is it worth not obeying God?

6. After reading this chapter, what is one thing you will put into practice or one thing you will change in your life?

7. How can we, as a group, help you do this?

Chapter 9

-Often believers face their greatest spiritual _____ after their greatest _____.

-Allow God to give you a renewed sense of _____ so that you can continue to ride or die in the face of your _____.

-God calls us to ride and die for Him, but He also call us to ride and die _____.

-Elijah was not alone, and _____ are _____!

What is your biggest area of discouragement?

Write down three actions you can take to overcome your discouragement:

1.

2.

3.

Group Study Questions:

1. How does discouragement affect our ability to ride or die?

2. How can we guard against discouragement after we experience a spiritual victory?

3. How do we get our eyes off of everything that leaves us shaken and get focused on the peace of God? What are some practical ways to do this?

4. Why is it important to have friends? Do you have friends you can rely on in your life?

5. Why is it important to know other men are serving God?

6. After reading this chapter, what is one thing you will put into practice or one thing you will change in your life?

7. How can we, as a group, help you do this?

Chapter 10:

-In their moment of death, they chose to stand with God and not deny Him. They _____ on God for help, and He gave them the _____ they needed.

-Jesus tells us to_____ our enemies. We must _____ for them. It isn't easy, but it's part of being a ride or die follower of Christ.

Write down three things that stood out to you the most in this chapter:

1.

2.

3.

Group Study Questions:

1. How are Christians in America experiencing persecution today?

2. How are we suppose to handle it when the world persecutes us?

3. Why is it important to show love and forgiveness to those who persecute us?

4. This goes against our natural tendencies. How do we practically do it?

5. After reading this chapter, what is one thing you will put into practice or one thing you will change in your life?

6. How can we, as a group, help you do this?

Chapter 11:

-It is impossible to live as a strong Christian if you are not
_____ _____'s _____.

- _____ should always be a result of reading
God's Word. This allows God's Word to _____ us
and make us more like _____.

-We need to stop making _____ for our sin and
compromise and go to _____ in passionate
obedience to God.

Do you struggle to read the Bible daily? Why?

What was the last thing God convicted you for in your life while
reading the Word?

What steps did you/can you take to make changes? Be extreme like Josiah.

1.

2.

3.

Group Study Questions:

1. Be honest: How often do you read the Bible?

2. This chapter states: *"It is impossible to live as a strong Christian if you are not reading God's Word."* Do you agree with this? Why or why not?

3. What was the last thing you felt convicted of while reading the Bible? Did you repent and make a change?

4. Josiah was EXTREME in his obedience. What action can you take to be EXTREME in your obedience to God's Word?

5. Will you commit to reading God's Word daily? (You should take advantage of Mantour Ministries' Year-Long Bible Plan, available in print format as well as a free email format.)

6. After reading this chapter, what is one thing you will put into practice or one thing you will change in your life?

7. How can we, as a group, help you do this?

Conclusion:

-As you daily choose to live with a ride or die attitude, you could be the _____ future _____ admire.

A personal note from Jamie:

I believe in you. I believe that you have what it takes to be a ride or die man of God. I believe that you have the strength to do whatever God asks of you, to go wherever He leads, to stand firm against anything and everything the world throws at you. You have what it takes to follow God, to pick up your cross, to ride or die for God no matter what! God can use your ride or die life and inspire another man to do the same. You have what it takes! Commit yourself to ride or die, no matter what!

-Jamie Holden

Will you accept the challenge of this book and and Ride or Die with God?   If so, state so below:

I, _____ declare today that I accept the challenge to ride or die with God. I will obediently follow Him as I work to fulfill His purpose for my life. I will overcome whatever personality traits or weaknesses I have to ride or die. I will follow Him in faith, resolving to stand firm. No matter what the world or the enemy throws at me or what discouragement I will face, I will ride or die with Him. Even if it brings persecution, I will ride or die in love as I wholeheartedly serve God. I will read and obey His Word, allowing the Bible to convict me and lead me to make

changes in my life. God has called me to ride or die with Him, and today I choose to answer His call!

_____   _____

           Signature   Date

Group Study Questions:

1. After reading through this book, what does the phrase *Ride or Die* now mean to you?

2. How will your decision to ride or die affect future generations?

3. Will you decide that there is nothing God could ask of you that you would not be willing to do?

4. If it means you will go to the ends of the earth for God and taking risks for Him, will you stand by Him and for Him no matter the cost?

5. Will you ride with Him even if it ends up killing you?

6. Will you make a statement of extreme loyalty and devotion to God, no matter what He does, where He leads, or what He asks of you?

7. After reading this conclusion, what is one thing you will put into practice or one thing you will change in your life?

8. How can we, as a group, help you do this?

FILL IN ANSWERS

Chapter One:

- committed, follow, ride, die
- tough, get riding,

Chapter Two:

- filth, sin
- no matter what
- next generations victories

Chapter Three:

- admitting, forgiveness, devoting
- hold nothing back

Chapter Four:

- talents, abilities, further God's
- persecution, strength, do, mission
- eternal consequences

Chapter Five:

- get out, He asks
- promised, love
- love, trust, loyal

Chapter Six:

- follow, obey
- say, do, God's
- woke, firm, honor

Chapter Seven:

- religion, idol
- not to bow
- leave, forsake

Chapter Eight:

- attacks, victories
- purpose, discouragement
- together
- neither, you

Chapter Nine:

- depended, strength
- love, pray

Chapter Ten:

- comfort, highway option
- tendencies, struggles

Chapter Eleven:

- reading God's Word.
- Repentance, change, Jesus
- excuses, extremes

Conclusion:

- legend, generations

Bibliography

Chapter One

* TobyMac, "Ignition" Portable Sounds, ForeFront, February 2007.

1. "ride or die." Dictionary.com. dictionary.com, LLC, 2011. https://www.dictionary.com/e/slang/ride-or-die/. Accessed: 30, August 2021.

2. "ride or die." urbandictionary.com. Urban Dictionary, 1999-2021. https://www.urbandictionary.com/define.php?term=ride%20or%20die, Accessed: 30 August 2021.

Chapter Three

1. A Summer Romance. Directed by: David Winning, Writer: Robert Tate Miller, performances by: Erin Krakow, Ryan Peavey, Sarah Strange, Crown Media Productions, 2019, Film.

Chapter Four

1. Arterburn, Steve, Stoeker, Fred. "Every Man's Challenge: How Far Are You Willing To Go For God?", Colorado Springs, Co, WaterBrook, May 18, 2004

Chapter 7

1. "resolve." Dictionary.com. dictionary.com, LLC, 2011. https://www.dictionary.com/browse/resolve. 30 August 2021.

* Cooper, John. Cooper Stuff, https://cooperstuffpodcast.com/.

2. Dorman, Steve. "SCOTUS decision on refusing service to same-sex couple was 'devastating,' Christian florist says", Fox News. July 15, 2020, https://www.foxnews.com/faith-values/christianflorist-scotus-decisiondevastatingfbclid=IwAR1xhLSOvlslJWPtnkv9Ztb_8-8_TbP Ph5d4Ym0BbhA0sSvPAP71G5uP044, Accessed July 30, 2021.

Chapter Nine

1. Washington Area Coalition of Men's Ministries. (XXX). WHY MEN MATTER - BOTH NOW AND FOREVER A Look at the Numbers Acessed: bout Men and Men's Ministry, http://www.wacmm.org/Stats.html   Accessed: 30 August 2021.

2. Capra, Frank, Frances Goodrich, Albert Hackett, Jo Swerling, James Stewart, Donna Reed, Lionel Barrymore, Thomas Mitchell, Henry Travers, Beulah Bondi, Gloria Grahame, and Philip V. D. Stern. Frank Capra's It's a Wonderful Life. United States: Republic Entertainment, 1998.

Chapter Eleven

1. Roach, David. "Bible Reading Drops During Social Distancing", Christianity Today, July 22, 2020, https://www.christianitytoday.com/news/2020/july/state-of-bible-reading-coronavirus-barna-abs.html Accessed: 30 August 2021.

2. LifeWay Research. "State of the Bible" (January 19, 2020) http://lifewayresearch.com/wp-content/uploads/2019/07/Discipleship-Pathway-2019-Engaging-the-Bible-Release.pdf Accessed: 30 August 2021.

3. Captain America: Civil War. Directed by Russo, Anthony, Joe Russo, Writer: Christopher Markus, Stephen McFeely, Kevin Feige, performances by: Chris Evans, Robert Downey, Scarlett Johannson, Sebastian Stan, Anthony Mackie, Don Cheadle, Jeremy Renner, Chadwick Boseman, Paul Bettany, Elizabeth Olsen, Paul Rudd, Emily VanCamp, Marisa Tomei, Tom Holland, Marvel Studios, 2016. Film.

ALSO AVAILABLE FROM MANTOUR MINISTRIES

Burning Daylight

The Godly Man's Call To Rise and Shine

Whatever It Takes

Living A Life Worthy Of Your Calling

Under Construction

We're All Men Under Construction!

INVINCIBLE

You've Stayed At Your Mountain Too Long!

Get In The Game

It's Time To Get Out Of The Locker Room and Get In The Game!

Legacy: Living A Life That Lasts

How Will You Be Remembered?

PUTTING ON MANHOOD

IT'S TIME TO PUT ON GODLY MANHOOD!

Will You Partner With Me To Reach Men With The Gospel?

Pray

Please pray for me as I work to reach men inside and outside of the church with the life-changing truth of the Gospel.

Give

Will you consider partnering with me on a monthly basis? Give online at www.giving.ag.org and enter my account number 2813962

Go

Plan to attend your local Mantour Conference.

Jamie Holden
US Missionary Assoc.   Account Number 2813962

GOD IS DOING A MIGHTY WORK IN MEN, YOUR SUPPORT HELPS US FULFILL HIS CALL!

U.S. Missions Faith Promise

Assemblies of God U.S. Missions • 1445 N. Boonville Ave. • Springfield, MO 65802–1894
Phone: (417) 862–2781, ext. 3264 • Fax: (417) 873–9734 • email: AGUSMFinance@ag.org

DONOR INFORMATION

Church   Individual

Name

Address

City   State   Zip

Email   Phone

Account number   Church to credit

Check here if you do not wish to receive promotional materials from U.S. Missions

RECIPIENT INFORMATION

As the Lord enables us, we promise to invest $_____ each month for support of:

Name of account: James J. Holden

Account #: 2813962   Department: Church Mobilization

Donor Signature   Date

IMPORTANT: Sign, date, and mail this form today along with your first check, or manage your giving online at www.giving.ag.org. At your faith promise is an agreement between you and God, it is understood that you may revise your promise at any time. God bless you!

U.S. MISSIONS

FORWARD TO AGUSM

**You Can Give Online At:
www.giving.ag.org**

I'd love to come share a challenging word of victory!

DEFEAT IS NOT AN OPTION!

CONTACT ME TO COME SHARE.

Jamie loves to speak to men and is available to speak at your next men's event. Jamie combines humor and his personal testimony to both engage and challenge men to grow in their walk with God. He uses his testimony of overcoming abuse as well as dealing with his physical and emotional issues growing up to encourage men that no matter what their background or where they have come from in life, they can grow into mighty men in God's kingdom.

"Years ago, while I was attending the University of Valley Forge, God gave me a deep desire to minister to men. My calling is to help men learn what it means to be a godly man and how to develop a deep, personal relationship with their heavenly Father. We strive to challenge and encourage men to reach their full potential in God's kingdom."

If you are interested in having Jamie at your next men's event as a speaker or workshop leader, or if you are interested in having him come share with your church, e-mail him at jamie@mantourministries.com. He is also available to speak for one or multiple weeks on the theme of his books, Burning Daylight, Whatever It Takes, Invincible: Scaling The Mountains That Keep Us From Victory. Putting On Manhood, Legacy: Living a Life that Lasts, and Get in the Game.